Bards Annual 2020

The Annual Publication of the
Bards Initiative Long Island

Bards Initiative

James P. Wagner (Ishwa)—Editor, Compiler

Nick Hale—Submissions Editor, Compiler

Marc Rosen—Associate Editor

J R Turek—Associate Editor

Cover Art: Vincent (VinVulpis) Brancato

Layout Design: James P. Wagner (Ishwa)

Published by Local Gems Press

www.localgemspoetrypress.com

<u>Bards Initiative Staff</u>

President

James P. Wagner (Ishwa)

Vice President

Nick Hale

Treasurer

Marc Rosen

Council

Jillian Wagner

Ed Stever

Margarette Wahl

Sharon Anderson

Kate Fox

Ryan Jones

Douglas G. Swezey

Foreword

2020 is the 10th anniversary of Bards Annual, it has also been a year with some unique challenges. The world was hit out of nowhere with an unprecedented level of shut downs that we haven't seen on this scale in human history. Suddenly so many things were uncertain, so many things were up in the air, events that had been planned for months or even years needed to be cancelled or postponed, and April, poetry month, had to be shifted to a virtual environment. But we did it. We made it work.

I remember early on during the crisis, only a couple of places were offering virtual poetry events. As I write this, I get over 30 invites to such events a day, no longer limited by geography the options have become plentiful. For our part at Local Gems Press and the Bards, we put up a website to host an online poetry convention, and thousands flocked to it-from poetry communities across America and beyond. We did virtual workshops, the results of some becoming best-selling books on Amazon, we hosted interviews and provided free eBooks. Poets from different corners of the country and globe--many whom had never met, starting writing collaborative poetry together, connecting, creating, forming new virtual communities.

And now, books that were postponed are starting to happen again. Launch events are trickling back, and as always, we will overcome. We are resilient; Poets and creators especially so. There is always a silver-lining, during this time of hardship many of us learned and adapted to various new forms of technology that can spread our poetry even further. And of course, this will only add to the already rich tradition of live gatherings to hear poets perform that has gone back over 6000 years.

~ James P. Wagner (Ishwa)

Table of Contents

Lloyd Abrams

when i fell in love

a warm september sunday
a drive to the cloisters
lush surroundings
stained glass windows
the unicorn tapestry
and you're wearing
that blue miniskirt
oh … my … lord

then left-arming it in my '68 chevelle
with my right cuddling you real close
down the elevated west side highway
with the windows rolled down
and wnew-fm up high
through the tunnel to the gowanus to the belt
then into that tiny roadside parking strip
under the verrazzano bridge
where i just couldn't
get enough
of you

it was then
that it hit me
and i knew
that you …

you were the one
for me

– for Vivien, my devil in a blue skirt … and still, after fifty plus years

Sharon Anderson

An Opportune Season

They call this the season of giving.
I ask why giving,
caring, helping others,
requires a season?

He didn't choose a season
to lose his job, his home,
his family.

She didn't choose a season
to find herself asking
for change from strangers;
seeking shelter in subways,
wearing threadbare cast-offs,
eating from dumpsters.

Homelessness
doesn't have a season.

Hunger
doesn't have a season.

Hopelessness
doesn't have a season.

Why is it that we choose to wait
to offer sustenance, support, shelter
until it is the season?

Rose Anzick

Attitude

I have an attitude
I can't tell you the latitude
I am not being rude
It is making me crude
There is the gray sky
It makes me want to cry
Being in quarantine
I just want to scream
The virus
Is upon us
No place to go
Except to and fro
Can’t let it get to me
Hopefully soon we will be free

William Balzac

Words

If Words ever mattered,
Let me speak these:
I was Here,
When each word
Was more than a Tweet.

What was said
You could hold in your Hand,
Your Heart.

Goodness clings
To each Word, we've learned.

Thus,
Their Value,
Can never be forgotten,

Because
I was Here,
In this moment
With You.

Antonio Bellia (Madly Loved)

Patriarchs, then Ragout

The Patriarchs are gone.
All gone.
The Patriarchs are
All gone.

With them they
Have taken judgment,
And solutions,
Influence, and
Accountability.

The Patriarchs are
Not there,
Are not there to
Praise or condemn.

Relieved somewhat
We could have run
Free
And perhaps, then,
Astray.

But no.
They left behind the Matriarchs,

Who continued to administer
All the teachings the
Fathers taught, and also
All the words that
For manhood's sake
They could never say.

But also with
Elixir of ragout,
With perfect
Table set
For Sunday dinner,
Got us all back
With attention doubled.

Now the Matriarchs
Are going.
Alone, in dismay
We think
Who will be the
Patriarch in charge?
Who will gently
But firmly
Administer words
Of wisdom
On Sundays, with
An inebriating and
Convincing elixir of
Ragout?

Cristina Bernich

the bird

Bones buzzing, humming, standing on tip toes.
Stuck, pulling, wriggling away, desperation must not show.
Voices murmur, distant echoes, as I am caged again.
Nothing clear, crisp, vivid, all muted and dull, colors blend.
Clarity faded so slowly these years, I never knew, until I felt
that urging buzz,
in my bones of the hard wrong all that this was.
I no longer know the self I see.
Delicate bird, bones nervous, helpless, belonging to the sky,
but locked within bars the strongest spirit hopeless to pry.
Edge of hunger growing too sharp, a punctuated rip.
Louder those whispers, pleading "Go, go, between those bars
just slip."
Growing inside, erupting, a torrid so violent,
the idea swells and pours over, no longer silent.
Searing ache to be where I can take flight,
to see again clearly, not bound and locked in this seesaw fight.
Stand on that precipice, teetering on my choice,
a choice *because,* not *despite.*
Bursting to go, smothered one more time, barred again by
your ***NO.***
Deep brown eyes close, caught again and taking it,
the will you think I relinquish, replenished, these eyes do not
forget.

Blinded by your arrogance, you cannot see my feathers beneath your wide, rough hands.
So from bruised knees, again,
I rise.
I stand.
You cannot see the shining brilliance of it all, as these hollow bones escape and fly to the sun.
My choice made, it was never yours, and it cannot be undone.
The cliff will be air, falling, clouds push to the sky.
Bird bones humming, carried away, I fly.
Voices nudge me forward, whispers feed me to the sun,
shining warm on a creature free,
endless blue air, breathe deep, vivid crisp, sweet jubilee.
Carry my soul, like wisps of breath, carry me from my silent captivity.

Thérèse M. Craine Bertsch

Desire

I am 80 years old
but I recall being here
The chill on a cool spring day
empty of companions

Solitary and satisfied
I am content wearing my nice cashmere sweater
A Christmas gift
no one here to wear it for

This place smells of the sea
every breeze carries her beautiful scent
There are no questions
just loneliness and longing

We are made for love
I remember this place

Damien Bettinger

comfort is an expression

fresh directions the heart takes us on
beat by beat
every 8th note fills the body
with a mindful sense of spirit
can you hear it?
recalling a way back towards source
experiencing the illusion of Death as though it were a
transformation of the force
truly observing everything within our means...
best interests settle in the qualities we redeem...

situations have sides
decisions effect lives
transmissions alter vibes
and reception becomes one's guide

seek a better way
to ease stress
and refuse to let uncertainty
lay one's ambitions to rest

ask questions, offer reflections, and extend one's connections...

"comfort is an expression"

John A. Brennan

Worms

A round, rusted tin can, contents long ago devoured, sat in patient
silence on the sloped window sill.
The long-necked spade lounged like a bored corner-boy, against
the kitchen wall, waiting.
Hickory handle, time shaped by the grip of calloused hands,
stained with the spit of generations.
The blade, honed with a degree of perfect angle, ready to slice
deep in the dark loam and uncover the
life beneath the surface. Foot planted firmly on the lug, driven
deep, sod turned, sharp tap with the back
of the blade revealed earthworms, black-heads and from under the
roots of the dock, the trout's favorite,
fat, white grubs. Layer of soil in the can, a bed for the worms,
where squirming equality reigns.

Alice Byrne

Thaw

Something thawed in my house today.
The house where my soul lives
In that deep frozen locker that has been my broken heart ,something thawed.
I emphasize seemed.
Seemed to thaw,not sure yet.
A spring melt,a solstice of sorts.

I marched across the Siberian desert with Stalin's exiles
Then you found me and I smiled.
A moistness on my heart's surface.
Something awoke in my soul that I thought had been completely devoured by the soul vampires.
And my mind lightened.
Something sprouted.
And I thank you for your love.
I return it.

Carlo Frank Calo

Ouroboros

The gaping jaws of life beckon,
But is it to free or enslave,
The twisting gut poised,
Now receiving, now expelling,
Like a bull and a bear,
Charging out, hibernating in,
As life goes on eternally,
The first cry of a baby,
The last breath of an old, old man.

Paula Camacho

#143

-after William Shakespeare

I run away from the housewife inside
fling the feather duster to the wind
set down the baby to make a mad dash
in pursuit of the thing I would desire.
My neglected child follows my movements
his cries like a net that flings out to me
to catch what remains of my soul
and I cannot escape the thing inside
that would hold me against my will
the instinct of love lingering there.
But for the constant generational heredity
perhaps another day awaits somewhere
far into the future where I will come to miss
the warm soft peach of his skin against my kiss.

Lynne Cannon

Who knew you would be right?

once I thought I would be alone
and you said we should go
to that cartoon festival
down in the Village
and I thought no
but we did

I said, oh horrors, no minivan
but you said please
and we traveled
and the kids
sang along
with us.

I said if you turn into your father
and I turn into my mother
this could be terrible
but here we are
and we are
still us,
my love.

Patrick J. Cauchi

In huts and hospitals around the
world;
thousands, perhaps millions, are
away from stars.

Swept away by tsunamis of neglect
and ignorance.
Respirator snug in its plug;
electric breath;
not natural, verses a maleficent
virus, as natural as soil;
as black as plague;
Bubonic in purpose;
away from stars. . .
I cannot swallow.

Caterina de Chirico

Veteran's Day

We didn't know the letters PTSD
We didn't have 10K runs, fund raisers or service dogs,we didn't know what was wrong. The wives and kids of military men from WW II never knew why their husbands and fathers were sick , their bodies looked so fit.

We didn't know why they couldn't sit with their backs to a door or couldn't stand loud noises and firecrackers on the fourth, why they couldn't sleep or be in crowds or weren't able to speak about simple things at the dinner table .

No one told us what was wrong when the ambulance came to our door to take him away year after year on Independence Day, they said it was Malaria or Rheumatic fever, they didn't know PTSD either .

Although he went to work each day we didn't have enough to pay the bills, that was our little secret behind closed doors along with the skeletons in the closet from the SS Saratoga, IwoJima and Okinawa .

We heard about Guadalcanal, the Bridge over the River Kwai and the Japs and the Japs and the dead friends in fox holes, but we never heard about PTSD.

Some said it was “ shell shock “ and it would get better, but it never did, it only got worse for a Brooklyn kid who dreamt of running away to San Francisco to protest the war with flowers in her hair, running as fast as her skates could fly from the nightmares,late night fights and the blasting noise of the TV to hide
the screaming threats to kill with a knife, night after night after night .

Relief finally arrived in the summer of 69 when he died.They said it was cancer but we knew it was suicide .

No one told us what was wrong, we didn’t know the letters PTSD,we didn’t have 10 K runs, fund raisers or service dogs, we didn’t know how cruel war was for the little ones now all grown up, who listen to politicians wage endless war and thank the military for their service .

Anne Coen

Poetry in Season

When poets meet in the produce aisle at Trader Joe's,
we don't gripe about grapes.
There is no banana banter.
Even sweet corn fails to make us swoon.

Our eyes lock on the display of plumcots and apriums.
Transfixed, we say their names over and over,
letting the sound ripen on our tongues.

We debate whether plumcots can be safely consumed on
hammocks,
fantasize about serving apriums in atriums.

We're definitely clogging the aisle.
Soccer moms deftly maneuver strollers around us,
Elderly customers despair of reaching the checkout counter before
expiration dates.
The produce manager gives us a baleful eye.

Just as we're about to head to the register,
our mischievous friend Lloyd asks,
Have you tried the gourdomelons?

Joseph Coen

A Day in Paradise

Another day in paradise
Yet I am only half aware
Busy about something else
That really wasn't there
My best shot was in morning
Meditation sitting on my chair
Trying not to be distracted
Breathing in the air
Other moments were in day time
Focused on helping one prepare
Making the passage from this life
To the place beyond despair
Trying not judge others
In the store light's ugly glare
And remaining focused
On what and whom is in my care
Another day in paradise
But only half aware
All the way to heaven
Is the only way to get there

Jamie Ann Colangelo

My God, My Strong Tower

It was a beautiful day
Without a cloud in the sky
My sight extends far away
My spirit leaps to new highs

Suddenly, without warning
Shrouded in a cloud cover
A perfect storm was brewing
Ominous waves hover

The water bears down on me
Salty splashes burn my eyes
Vision gone, I cannot see
Will this – this - be my demise?

My heart's pounding, gripped by fear
Fiercely trembling, I cower
"Oh My God, My God, come near,
Gird me in Your strong tower"

Jane Connelly

The Screen Door

I sit at the back door with Luigi
My cat, who has aged along with me, and
Who may be the last of my pets
He stares out, as he often does, to the
Corner of the yard where his brother,
Aloysius, sleeps under the earth.

The statue I placed there looks
Exactly like him, and that was where
Luigi saw me carry him away
Out of the house we all shared for years.

As quickly as events change our lives
The weather changed overnight, and the
Wind is bending the tops of the sycamore trees
Back and forth, as if in prayer
Clapping the branches, and the colorful leaves
Are falling, falling
Covering the yard and the grave.

The wind rattles the screen door
And for a moment I think I hear Aloysious
Scratching at the screen door once again.

Lorraine Conlin

Imprimatur

Sundays after Mass I'd pour through pamphlets
books and Bibles sold in the back of our Church.
On the black wrought iron stand between
How to Pray the Rosary and *Shall I be a Nun*
I found the small book, *Dating for Young Catholics.*

My younger brother always questioned me about sex,
a subject I knew little about, so I thought it would be
a good purchase to share and learn about together.
The book, written by a Very Reverend Monsignor,
wasn't expensive so I slid the money into the cash box,
put the book in my purse and ran home to read it in the refuge
of my room.

It touched on necking, petting, drinking, driving,
smoking and going steady, all things I hoped to be doing
very soon.
I was out of the convent, in a co-ed high school
with no hands on knowledge or personal experiences to share
with my brother who was already "girl crazy"
and soon starting his freshman year at Christ the King
High School.

I sold him on the book, noting its approval by the Church,

pointed out the black cross symbol, (the *imprimatur*), proof a bishop endorsed it.
I reminded him the nuns stressed we look for these things when buying books suitable for good Catholics to read.

Nodding approval he tore it from my hands before I could say another word
ran into his room and shut the door.
He avoided me for several days and I thought perhaps he was embarrassed
and I should break the silence by asking him how he liked the book.

"Tommy, do you have any questions about what you read in the book?"
Just one. If a girl plays with herself, does it feel good?

I didn't read anything about that in the book and didn't know how to answer him.
I slept with my hands above the covers like the nuns said we should do.
But I blurted out a *YES* because I wanted him to think I knew the answer.

Ushiku Crisafulli

Stir crazy,
my mind's hazy.
Penned in like chicken
that never lays...
e-mergency broadcasts
and a merging of powers.

When did we surrender control of the supply chain?
I hear vegans got beef
with carnies,
but you can't get the show on an empty road.

Do we even know where our food is grown?
Butcher, cheesemonger, greengrocer, and farmer...
were stripped from our communities
as corporations got larger.

Do as thou wilt but no do harm,
surrounded by snakes...
surrender to charm.

We're distanced for awhile,
but community can return...
with fat and full hearts,
there's no thinning this herd.

Max Dawson

Imagination

Creatures of any make believe kind
That have formed in the confines of the human mind
Make believe names, powers, and places
Imagine angels, demons, and alien races
Fictitious people and sources of power
What view of what sort of kingdom can you imagine?
As you pretend to gaze out of the window of a grand tower
See to create your own philosophy, religion, and creed
Sometimes putting your imagination on paper can be a great deed
Can you imagine fiction itself into a story?
There have been those that have imagined their imaginations into glory

Anthony DeGennaro

Subterranean

Do you see my eyes
pupils wide, glass lakes of obsidian.
Can you hear my heart stop
and freeze time in its icy grip.

I know you can't see it yet.
It's subterranean,
budding like spring's first green
not an inch below the thawing winter muck.

Close, so very close,
you can feel its warmth on your skin
like the rising sun's rays
slicing through a cold blue morning frost.

I don't have to tell you what I've lost
you already know the cost.
But it will all be worth it - you'll see -
just wait a few more moments.

Debbie De Louise

Poetry Contest

Wrap words around a reader's mind
tie a magic bow on Pandora's box
open a vine branched door
flying carpets glide west
hot air balloons float south
wicked witch of the north
eastern winds scatter verbs
Peter Pan kidnaps Moby Dick
Imagination shares its kick
Close your eyes
blindfold pirates
step aboard the boats of nouns
compass points toward flower fields
rainbows burst in color shadows
pottery, pans, and pies
mix the batter with rhythmic spoons
pour the velvet into the sand
claim your prize.

Arlene Diaz

Almost Closing Time

Cheap whiskey in hand
Stale cigarette on lips
Skirt hiked up
Bad choices ready to be made
Swaying her way to the dance floor
Among the rest of the lost souls
Screaming to be needed like a bad habit
All the while cheap whiskey in hand
Stale cigarette on lips

Sharon Dockweiler

That Star to the Right

If I could I would dwell
Near that star to the right
On that misty soft planet
That's just out of sight

I'd gather your essence
And breathe you to life
And you'd be my husband
And I'd be your wife

We'd build a small house
In a lullaby tree
And eat of its fruits
With a view of the sea

We'd cultivate melons
Build fires, bake yams
You'd sing to our daughters
By fields of blue lambs

But that star's out of reach
And I don't feel you near
And no trees here sing lullabies
Into my ear

So I watch all the others
Who live life in pairs
And say that I'm grateful
As I climb the stairs

And see out the window
That star to the right
Near that misty soft planet
That's just out of sight.

Joseph Drouin-Keith

Praises of the Robin

The small Robin, delicate and free
Makes its home in the densest tree.
Gardener's friend, for ages long
Tweets a sweet melody, a beautiful song.
Digging the silt, the dirt, the grime
To grow the new chicks, to give them mealtime.
Alone in the world, without family nearby,
Only one of its kind, yet flying free in the sky.
With sturdiest love, protecting its young
Keeping broods safe until its life is done.
Well remembered, shown by names untrue
Fools the common folk despite dissimilar coo.
Stunning red breast, a small, fluffy ball
Like a winged sheep, fluffed up by nightfall.
Kindness from diggers and farmers abounds
When disturbing plants' dirt, the richest of grounds.
Bird of tradition, from Christian to Norse
Helping the people with kindness, not force.

Mike Duff

Snarky Moon

Snarky moon,
hiding changes of expression behind clouds
that hie away summer and summon the chill,
watching us take out our winter wardrobe
and sigh away shorts to couture confinement,
beaming,
slowly winding away,
leaving us to our fate
aglow in its mother's attention,
pock-marked, beshadowed,
imagined dentation wearing away in consideration,
and its time in courtship wearing away.
What does the moon know?
What do the whipping whispy clouds
Reveal?
Expressions shocked, stunned
amused, bemused,
sad-eyed and smirking.
What do I conceive when I see the moon?
That even things that return grow farther way
as I, too, slip deeper into time
and beyond all appraisal.

Peter V. Dugan

The tapestry

montage of color
pattern of culture
contrast and compliment

the finest linen,
the coarsest burlap
bits of silk,

shards of denim,
rags and remnants
woven, spun, bound

together, individual
cuts of cloth
a quilt

neglected
worn fabric
split seams

tension and stress
tear apart the stitching
rending the design

restoration, preservation
for future generations
or hemmed up, bordered,

a relic, the peace
this piece
of Americana

Alex Edwards-Bourdrez

Early Morning On 5th Avenue

It was a most elegant accident,
A majestic, fast, and graceful
Airborne tumble of cyclists
In the extended rest of a symphony score
After the timpani roll of wheels
Against the yellow taxi's door.

Tremulous stillness started the next movement:
Leaves in the morning breeze down the avenue,
As smooth as the olympian bodies
Curled in a soft and silent landing,
Unfolding then standing and sporting
Smiles as playful as the shimmering sunlight.

Darlene Famiglietti

The Trail

Step onto the trail
amid the noise,
the traffic,
the electric hum,
the worry,
the regret,
the chatter in your mind.
Step by step
it melts away,
until the only noise you hear
is your footsteps on a carpet of pine needles,
the call of birds,
the rush of wind,
the distant train whistle.
Step by step
until silence surrounds you.
Step by step
until calmness wraps around you.
Step by step
until your mind stills.
Deeper into yourself.
Deeper into your heart.
Step by step
until all you feel is
peace.

Donna Felton

The kids.....

The kids are getting antsy
I am bored is what they say
Moving all around the house
Inside is hard to stay
Another plate, another dish
Out of oreos and goldfish
Soup, sandwiches and cookies
Do you want to bake?
Parents everyone saying
How much can we take?
Uno, Candyland and Scrabble
And then a tick tock dance
A moment to yourself
If you get the chance
Connect four, and Monopoly are
Spread across the floor
Mothers everywhere scream
We can't take no more!
Questions that they are asking
Some don't have a clue
So we try and keep busy
And do what they want to
Just dance, now Lizzo

its my turn to sing
Just being with our babies
We can get through anything!!!

dam D. Fisher

Nothing To Fear

The condo hires a man
with a border collie
who runs around the pond
to frighten geese away.
Two geese fly off
but the remaining twenty
paddle calmly
in the center of he pond.
When the dog runs
to the eastern shore, the geese
move slightly to the west
and when he runs to the west
they move slightly to the east.
This goes on four or five times.
The dog's tongue is
hanging out and his pace
slowed.

I cheer and root for the geese.
When the dog plunges into the water
the geese hiss and honk, flap their wings
scaring him off. Geese like swans
harass anyone who comes near.

Melissa E. Filippelli

cry

cold, beyond tired
filled with noise
Creator, help me
keep my poise
aching heart
arrogant desire
fill me
with a holy fire
done trying
beyond grief
help me, oh help me
in my unbelief
joyless participant
buried in time
keep me kind
hurried
haggard
ready to weep
will someone
please
show me how to see

Finally, the geese tire
of the game and fly off
but soon return.

Denise-Marie Fisher

Brushstrokes

Her hair was long and coarse;
a multicolored gray
with soft highlights of white
and dimensional,
due to the darker tones.

Upswept into a knot
it cascaded nicely,
held together by one
solitary hair pin-
amazingly enough.

Her eyes were softer now,
their vibrant brown toned down
and her pallor more pink.
In her days of sunshine
she glowed and glistened tan.

Lipsticks in pale colors
replaced the oranges
and the reds- she was wise
enough to know the time
to leave the harsh colors.

She reached to brush her hair
but found her arms too weak.
She held the brush to me…
and as the strands slipped through,
I heard her sigh softly.

Kate Fox

show me

don't tell me
what you
used to have
used to do
used to be

don't tell me
what you're
gonna do
gonna have
gonna be

show me
who you are
and
what you're
about

the rest of it?
you're just
flap
flap
flapping
your
gums

Glenn P. Garamella

Snowfall

Outside the bedroom window,
a fist of ice choked the mouth of the drainpipe.
Last night it snowed as night dreamed its dream
and the backyard woke in a white winter blanket.

The morning was quiet inside and outside
the stone walls of the house,
nothing moved except a shaft of light
where dust swirled like stars in a slow tornado.

I could feel my heart beat and hear the fridge hum,
the cat buried itself along the hissing radiator
the floor was too cold for bare feet.

The day began as the day begins,
there was not much to do
except carry this body from room to room.

Couldn't think of going outside
so I watched the snow melt off the roof
in thin ropes of summer rain;
one could almost forget the name of the season.

George S. George

Willow

This Weeping Willow needs dropping in the sea,
for the sea is balm to the crying of the land
and has a heaving surge of joy unlike
the sad drooping of trees.
Leaves fallen into streams are deceived not unto death,
for they ride, aye they ride, the river tide to frolic
in the pounding, fisted surf…
And where is the rain-drenched death-rot then?
Salt preserves.
A Thousand
            Thousand
                        Rain
                              Tongues
Tempt
      This
            Sea-dreaming
                              Tree
Come home with us to the singing sea;
Your long-armed sisters wait for thee.
For though I have seen the moonlit water wait
And have heard the sighing of the tree,
Mocked by the bright eyes of mole and mate,
I am not the one can set the willow free.

Tina Lechner Gibbons

Just Out of Reach

Every now and then
I find myself
Wandering the mall of memory
I stop in one of the shops
I pass along the way
Hidden far away, in a
Dark corner
I find a shelf marked
Tina's hopes and dreams
But it is high and out of
My reach
If I try to reach them
They will come crashing down
And shatter at my feet.
Perhaps they are best left
Out of my reach
That can stay intact
That way, if I have them
I can still believe that someday
I may actually have them
That Someday
Someone might get them down off the shelf
And hand them to me
Giftwrapped.

Jessica Goody

Fallen Apples

Ripe fruit dangles overhead like ornaments
tucked amidst shining leaves, greenly-scented,
dappling the lawn like an underwater sun.

Stumbling over the sharp stones of fallen apples
strewn among the tousled carpet of grass,
stems bitter with sap snapping under the weight

of their solid green heft, rustic baskets filling
with plops and thuds, and the mingled shades
of green: the green boulders of fallen apples

nestled in the roughness of damp grass;
lawn and leaves and piled fruit, crisply bitten
and running juice, bittersweet and glowing green.

Aaron Griffin

Essential

Unemployment doesn't scare me.
I never worked a day in my life.
All I've ever done is exploit the kindness of those who have more than me.
Those who actually worked.
You see, I've got this scheme going,
It's ingenious, and I don't know how I get away with it,
Where every morning at 4 AM, I force myself out of bed,
Then drive a half hour to a members – only warehouse club,
I put on a green apron, oversee the delivery of a truckload of produce,
Write the day's date on every single box,
Lift the 30 pound bags of potato and onions onto their own pallet,
Re-stack a couple dozen crates of bananas to allow the ethylene gas to escape,
Move the oranges, plums, peaches, apples, mushrooms into cold storage,
Then process several pallets of the older food to be donated to a food bank,
Then make sure the refrigerators and tables are clean and ready for the new stock to be rotated in.
Lug a pallet size crate of watermelons to the front door for the remote display,
Then go back and check everything I put out for sale for any signs

of spoilage.
There's more to it of course, as that list only accounts for what needs to be done before we open for the day.
There's baling cardboard, collecting shopping carts from the parking lot, sanitation sweeps, and a lot more.
But anyway, all I have to do, is all that, for 40 hours or more each week, and then at the end of the week, these suckers at the ware house club actually pay me money for it.
I mean, it isn't a lot of money, and it's buying power is only a fraction of what my parents were earning for similar jobs when they were my age, but hey, its money, and I didn't even have to work for it!
I've worked out one hell of a swindle.
Or at least the men on cable news said so.
You see, somehow or another, they figured me out.
They know I don't work for a living.
Work means sitting in a cushioned chair behind a computer in an air conditioned room, they say.
Anything where you have to stand, or get dirty, or exert physical effort of any kind, that ain't work, they said.
Those aren't real jobs. Those tasks are meaningless, unimportant, just diversions for high school kids to earn pocket money.
It's true, they say, that however strange it may be that these businesses have employees on duty during school and night hours when kids are under curfew, and that a great deal of those jobs require the use of equipment that you need to be an adult to legally operate.
But forget all that, they're men on television, so they have to be right.
Right?

In other countries, they say, people don't even get paid for what I do.
So I should be grateful to get any money for my menial, useless, disposable job at all, they said.
If I want to have my basic needs met, I should go get a real job, a respectable job, something where I have to wear a tie, and get as signed a cubicle, and partake in refined luxuries like hour-long lunch breaks, they said.
And a lot of the country agreed.
Then this virus started spreading, and suddenly I'm an "essential worker" to keep society operational?
Yeah, okay.
Sometime in the future, if this all blows over,
And these guys go back on cable news to call me "entitled" for thinking that working full time should earn me enough for pay for nutritious food, medical care, and a safe place to live, I'll remember this.
And we'll see who's "essential" then.

Valerie Griggs

At The Soup Kitchen

Darkness gets all over everything,
sticky, smudging.

Night pressing in, pushing down,
weighs like a regret,

the moon casts shadows
that crimp the heart.

Balancing moonlight on her apron,
eyes smiling into the longing,

the fallen woman wears the Milky Way
as she ladles home cooked charity,

bowl after bowl,
for her homeless neighbors.

Daryel Groom

Archangel of Peace

Great man of peace his voice echoing
Through generations of the racially
Oppressed
His voice bold yet compassionate
Will never cease to stir
The marginalized to strength and unification
His speeches like an angels symphony beckoning
The world to non-violent action
Against the unspeakable horrors of
Racism in a so called democracy
Freedom rings
Freedom rings
Let his words remind us of the fight for racial, ethnic, gender, and religious equality
His dream has become a nation's mantra
Let us honor Dr. Martin Luther King Jr. and all freedom
Fighters today and every day
By Daryel Groom

Maureen Hadzick- Spisak

Worm Moon 2020

As day slips to night
On the 9th of March
That orange disc seemingly
Perched in the trees
Is the March Worm Moon
So close to the Earth
It is also a super moon
The first super moon of 2020
The last full moon of winter

While you are looking up
The soil beneath your feet
Begins to soften
As the worms wiggle and jiggle
Up through the earth
Inviting the red red robin
To be the first
To snatch the early worm
And thus the Spring season begins

Geneva Hagar

There Are No Words

The day before started like the day before
coffee and the news, world news page A34.
In the left-hand corner column---
a virus was spreading over China.

The next day started like the day before
coffee and the news, world news page A24.
The ill had expanded overnight,
doubling up like wildfire.

The next day started like the day before
coffee and the news, world news page A4.
No boundaries could contain
the path of the invisible scourge.

The next day started like the day before
coffee and the news, world news page A1.
Delivery came in sinister silence,
one word, Pandemic, in large font.

Two arms apart became the normal,
together was yesterday,
upending life of all who knew it.
There are no words...

Nick Hale

Conspiracy Theory

The sun rises sideways
over an open harbor of
burning sails.
Fire sales.

Across the world,
somebody is building
a robot with two
left arms.

Bananas upside-down

The boss connects the dots.
This is how it's always been.

J. Peter Hansen

The Future Came Today

Woke up today and I was grateful
Woke up and everything had changed
Looked out my window, and it all looked the same
But life was forever rearranged

I never thought I'd see this moment
I never knew it would go this way
Where are the rainbows after the water
Somehow the future came today

Don't look back, looking for answers
The past has gone and faded away
Here and now, is all that's left to see
'Cause the future came today

What lies in store for us tomorrow
What will be left for us to hold
Looked at my mirror, and somehow something changed
And dreams would never turn to gold

Don't look back, looking for answers
The past has gone and faded away
Here and now, is all that's left to see
'Cause the future came today

Pray for miracles in my life
Pray for everyone
Day by day and every hour
Until the war is won

Don't look back, looking for answers
The past has gone and faded away
Here and now, is all that's left to see
'Cause the future came today

Here and now, is all we'll hope to be
'Cause the future came today

Michele Harber

The Search

Through the nighttime rides a soldier,
mounted on his steadfast horse.
A little grayer, somewhat older,
he plods along a charted course.

The road is long, the prey elusive.
Long he sought but ne'er he found.
The trail is hard and so abusive.
Still he rides toward higher ground.

Always aiming for the summit,
'though it seems so out of reach,
he gets so far, only to plummet,
in his search for lasting peace.

He searched throughout a Civil War
that didn't fulfill its name.
Civility went out the door,
while Atlanta was aflame.

Still he pursued his sacred dream,
through World Wars First and Second,
and all the battles to which, it seemed,
this poor soldier was beckoned.

His search took him to Korea,
and then on to Vietnam,
praying never again to see a
president who'd launch the Bomb.

He skirmished in the Middle East,
'though he didn't know what for,
nor why call them "skirmishes"; at least
be honest and call them war.

'Though he sees, with tired eyes blurred,
the path of devastation,
his quest for peace is undeterred
'midst wars without cessation.

Each new one that he's forced to see
is worse than the one before,
and he prays the next will fin'ly
be the war that ends all wars.

'Til then the lonely soldier rides,
through scenes of bloody battle,
the Angel of Death so near his side,
he hears its dark chains rattle.

Peace on earth, goodwill to man,
as ideals now seem defunct.
Beliefs they were the master plan
were summarily debunked.

And so the soldier plods along
atop his loyal steed,
wond'ring if we'll realize war is wrong
before others have to bleed.

Sylvia Harnick

Late Autumn

Endless days
of quiet grayness
deadened leaves
glued to unwashed
byways

harsh winds rustle
leafless trees
slanted rain splatters
on corrugated roof
play hypnotic
melodies

foggy mist
beclouds the
daylight muffles
sounds of falling
rain

Robert L. Harrison

The Poet Sport

The poetry reading
was dealt with
as an Olympic sport.
My friend who reads well
but cannot write
received three fives and a four.
The man with the deep voice
did better
and the mentor of the group
got four nines.
My turn would come next
would I have too much rhyme?
Would I be original and embrace
my play on words?
Now I stood before the judges
alone and ready to speak,
while watching their magic markers
put my poetry future down in numbers
on their score card.

Sheila Hoffenberg

The Joy of Laughter Amidst These Hard Times

What may seem funny to a person may not be the same to another
As we gather all insights of what the meanings are
Tears of joy, tears of sadness, they are all combined
The world has been hit with unpleasantness as we all know
But we are strong and will survive this outbreak
Just think that in nine months how many babies will be born
What else is there to do but be home and cuddle up with a loved one?
Many projects will get done, no more procrastination
Writing more, and reading, just think how much educated we will all be
Knowledge is in the core of our minds, deep into concentration
We prosper as we grow, we laugh at stupid things
We're amazed at the events taking place
Comedy and music is the best way to get through life
But right now, shows and events have come to a halt
So we must find ways to amuse ourselves
TV will bring us back to smiles
Just as long as it's not the news
It may seem like life's tribulations have gotten in the way
But just think of all the accomplishments we will take on
The future will put us on the right path
Where we will look back at all that's happened and laugh about it
We have to; we can't let this take us down

As long as we are healthy during this crisis
We will have that opportunity and we will endure
Just think about the good times, your children, grandchildren, your family and smile
Better yet, think of funny moments, what's the alternative?
Be happy and just LAUGH

Arnold Hollander

Nothing is Free

Nothing is free;
There's always a charge.
If it's not immediate,
Later on, it's quite large.

Pay when you enter
Or pay when you leave;
You won't escape,
There's no reprieve.

Any enjoyment
Comes with a price.
And the cost? Yes,
A throw of the dice.

So just remember
And take it from me;
Life is a struggle
And nothing is free.

Cheryl Huneke

The Many *Sides* of ME

Painting pictures from inspiration deep within my soul
Drawings flow from my thoughts and mind, then through my veins and down my fingers with pencil in hand onto paper transforming my ideas into dreams fulfilled.
Pen and ink are additives to enhance my paintings as needed, when inspiration hits.
Sewing flat fabrics of all kinds into three dimensional creations still have me in awe of the process each time I start and then complete a fabric project.
Gardening in the earths fertile dirt to bring flowers and beauty in some small way to my land.
Reading books that enhance my mind and create inspiration within.
Reading and writing poetry as I take in amazing words, that when put together to form a poem, move me in so many ways, that creating just pours out of me.
Reading anything and everything about almost anything, sinks into every tissue of my body, which then enhances the inspiration within me to bring out the motivation to create whatever wants to surface into an artistic way one of the many things I love to do and create.
I never know what side of me will surface, but when it does, I give it my ALL and passionately pursue my creation until it is com-

plete, and I see one of the many sides of me out in the open for a brief encounter with artistry in one of its many wonderful forms.

R. J. Huneke

I'm So Angry I Could . . .

I'm so angry I could . . .
Shoot a baseball
Smash knuckles into mulberry
Until cracking
Is bloody
Either the two inches of wood
Or hand
Are pulp

I'm so angry I could . . .
Send out silence
Ignoring all the protocols
To snub the fuck
Thieving prick
Blinded by greed and lack of
Kindness
The fuck

I'm so angry I could . . .
Spit on Batman
Snap all my pens and bleed 'em dry
Pulpy oozing
His bloody

Vessels are all torn open fresh
Spurting
I laugh.

Maria Iliou

Calling Home

Calling home
Calling heaven
Globally world wide
Sending message
Note of wording
Through breathe
In meditation

Up lifting virus
Is no longer serving us
Within people

Descending
Be observing
Within our inner self
Inner soul

Connecting
Connected open book

Revealing script

Chapter of isolation
Power of energy

Shifting altercation
Within power of
Universe

Tony Iovino

I Want to Drink with Hemingway

I want to drink with Hemingway,
A bottle of whiskey, maybe two
In the shade of an overhang outside
An old man's bar in the Keys
A lazy fan circling above us
As the blazing tropical sun fades
To an explosion of color to the West

I want to drink with Hemingway
A bottle of the house red, maybe two
At an umbrellaed table outside
A bookstore along the Seine
The shadow of Notre Dame before us
As the Parisian sky fades
To a pink only this city knows

I want to hear his secret treasures
Tales he denied his Royal Quiet Deluxe
Of seafaring voyages
Storms and fish and salt
Of weary war nights
Pain and fears and hope
Of dangerous foes
Bulls and sharks and women

I want to drink with Hemingway
A piping cup of sweet Café Cubano, maybe two
At an iron filigree round top for two outside
A café in the City of Columns
As we work through our hangovers
From the dark rum and the darker stories yet to be told.

Larry Jaffe

Ars Poetica

She found the crucible
of broken fate
a divine aesthetic
of ribboned notes

From the rubbish
she formed
a musical seascape
a symphony of color
a tapestry of sound

I beseech you
to call my name
in poetry
speak to me in verse
allow me entrance
to the sculpture

Lauren Jayne

The City By The Bay

I lost my true love in the pacific coast county
He was driving down a highway where the cliff meets the sea
Gonna bury his body by an old sycamore tree
His soul has gone to meet the Almighty

I'll pick wildflowers for his grave
Homeward bound through the central freeway
Now the golden gate of heaven is his final pathway
I lost him to the city by the bay

The stars shone like bright diamonds on that clear autumn night
But in the valley below a fog blocked the traffic light
When my love turned that corner the stop sign was out of sight
He didn't see the truck as it swerved to the right

I'll pick wildflowers for his grave
Homeward bound through the central freeway
Now the golden gate of heaven is his final pathway
I lost him to the city by the bay

Northern California Crash printed up in the news
A weather-related accident, no one to accuse
Both drivers were declared dead by the emergency crews
At their funerals, those crowds filled the chapel pews

I’ll pick wildflowers for his grave
Homeward bound through the central freeway
Now the golden gate of heaven is his final pathway
I lost him to the city by the bay

Jay Jii

Droplets of Late July

The alphabet
Fell from the sky
In a literary cloudburst

Quickly
I held out my cap
Snaring the wet letters
Within the reservoir
Of its discolored peak

Words and phrases
Began to emerge swiftly
Overflowing my shabby hat
And pouring to the ground
To form a deep puddle
Of regal poetry
At my feet

Sploosh...

Some days
Creating this
Is as effortless
As a promenade
In cool rain

Ryan Jones

Living Past

Who goes there
Who dares to enter this place
Hold your tongue
You must advance no further
Here it lies
The past, in heavy doses
It will wake
With the slightest error made
Watch your step

None but I
Live in this forsaken place
Here you are
The first to join me down here
Deep below
In the domain of the past
Passed away
And entombed here forever
Leave it be

Why you fool
You disobeyed my commands
To be still
And stay in utter silence

Now behold
The hungry past rests no more
No escape
It will take you for a ride
Through ruin

Fare you well
What you wish you could forget
You cannot
And now you will relive it
No mercy
The past is cruel and sharp
Like a knife
It cuts straight through to the heart
Relentless

Negative
Are the memories come back
Only these
Are what you must live again
What is more
Deeds you regret reoccur
Battles fought
Rage once more in great detail
No triumph

One more time
The deceased past has risen
It will hunt
Brace yourself for its onset

You have loosed
The most ancient of terrors
You set free
The ancestor of nightmares
Take the blame

Here it comes
I see you fading away
Off you go
It has gotten hold of you
Good luck friend
You will return a changed man
In knowledge
Of the past as you live it
In mourning

Daniel Kerr

The Big Chicken

If I was three inches taller,
had a bigger smile,
and spoke with a southern accent,
I would be my brother Charly.
If my moral compass was always true,
if I forgave more easily,
and spent more time helping broken human beings,
I would be my brother Charly.
If I burned down the woods when I was a little kid,
tried to put the fire out myself,
and then went to the police station to report it,
I'd be my brother Charly.
If I was a star football player in high school,
winning every game when I was a junior,
and losing every one when I was a senior,
I would be my brother Charly.
If I stopped other junior high kids from bullying the gay kid in
the 1960s,
shared a room with the first black football player at the Citadel
in the 1970s,
and today owned the only Chic-fil-A in North Carolina that
composes its waste,
I would be my brother Charly.
If I were a better Christian,
studied the bible regularly,
and volunteered to sit-in for caregivers so they could get a break,

I would be my brother Charly.
If I was Boy Scout leader most of my adult life,
guided countless Eagle scouts on their projects,
and took scouts camping when I was in my seventies when I had two bum knees,
I would be my brother Charly.
If I read more books,
took more walks on the beach,
and prayed more often,
I would be my brother Charly.
If I was always the last one off the plane,
because I helped the old ladies with their bags and young mothers with their babies,
and made sure to thank the pilot and all the flight crew before deplaning,
I would be my brother Charly.
If I provided a better example of a life well led,
and spread good will and humor,
with everybody I met,
I would be my brother Charly.
If I listened more,
spoke less,
and took myself less seriously,
I would be my brother Charly.
If I grew up in Alabama in the 1930s,
and a black man was falsely accused of raping a white woman,
and I had the courage and character of Atticus Finch to
defend him,
I would be my brother Charly.

Zach Klebaner

Departed Islands

On those days of dogma we sat
to craft waxen butterflies
that floated like origami in the wind
as the gamblers laughed
having been graced by a dealer of dreams.

At dawn we became elastic battleships
drifting parallel to possibility
and in the nights I dreamed
of cotton candy caves in a mountain of atrophy
of flamingos synthesizing electric epilepsy
of mimesis dead in the body of tomorrow.

When eternity collapsed the lobsters limped out
of the psoriatic sea to greet the sugared cows
grazing amidst the percolated immanence
and at your beckoning the coyotes came strolling
over the bagpipe hills with news of galactic alteration
that scribbled funerals to precious geometry.

Carissa Kopf

Unfolded Words

Pages crinkle as they turn
Emotions spark with every word
Tears spill and hearts break
Laughter pervades
Love elevates, higher than you can ever imagine
Anxiety builds within each page
Fingers linger under every word
Sometimes, demanding pause
Clutching the book tight to your chest

What kind of trip can we take
Between these bookcovers
Mysteries and secrets
Waiting for the right moment to unfold
Making us hold our breath
For the very next line
Characters come alive
Could they be evil
Who makes you angry and hateful
Maybe a romantic hero
Eliciting passion and lust

Therefore, we read
Unfolding the wonders of words

Going places to meet new faces
Feelings, exploring, living and hiding
Open a book
Weave through each chapter
Enjoy the creation
Of each amazing author
Out there in this world

Mindy Kronenberg

Siren Song

(after Ira Schneider's video, $H2O$ #22)

Can you hear my quick-silver lullaby
glimmering on the water's surface?
My head is a shell swollen with desire,
sweet briny dissonance calling
through a cacophony of clouds
to the water's persuasive
undulation.

Through shimmering light a storm
brews, stirs our maelstrom
of heartbeat and mayhem,
the wind's breath suddenly sliding
into thunder. We collapse
in a bubbled plume, cocooned
in the brackish depth of waves

until all you knew of childhood
dissolves, the life that lured you
to the open seas, bright horizons
tunneled into dark, the small
insistent voices from the past
shrinking to the curious silence
of release.

Melissa Kuch

Waiting

Alone, I wait fearful
as death is at my side,
with no one to comfort me
as my breath slowly subsides.

They say you come into this world alone
But still…

I heard my mother's heartbeat
I heard her voice so sweet,
like a lullaby from the unknown
I was never truly alone.

And as I lie here in silence
waiting for what is to come,
I can almost hear a gentle whisper
and a soft beating of a drum.

Because maybe there is a mother waiting
to place kisses on my cheek,
to hold me in her arms
and gently rock me to sleep.

I close my eyes and dream

there's a mother waiting in the unknown
and a father smiling lovingly
calling me home.

Joan Kuchner

The Dance

Catching the music,
my fingers thrum,
my thighs pulse,
my shoulders roll.
Inch by inch, I unzip my wrinkled skin
and jump onto the dance floor.
Young children join in the joy,
as their parents hide
embarrassment in conversation.
They have yet
to learn
to see
an ageless spirit
caught in the dance.

Jim Laino

To dream in the grove of the bemban palms

Crouched in the high grass clearing,
Where the river bends,
I hear the sonorous calls
of an unnamed clan.
Mud daubed and tattooed
Lurking amid the twisted mangroves
Wary as gazelles

I leave dark footprints through the cypress swamp
Where murmurs echo in pools of black water and
Mossy sloth hang upside down from vines,
Vacant yellow eyes
Betray no interest in my passing

Reaching the grove of the bemban palms
I enter to breathe their essence of wet cinnamon.
The witch of the grove rises from the roots
Like mist from a lagoon,
And finds the succor of my body.

She bids me to cool my back on her leathery bark,
And stretch my legs over fronds of soft fern.

In treetops
Parrots break the silence
Into many colors

Before my eyes close,
A brilliant paradise bird
Rises to the sun between the trees
Wings languidly waving goodbye to this world

My dream spirit rises from the forest floor
To follow him into the blue forever
Looking down, the treetops become a vast green sea
Butterflies dance on its surface
Like rainbow foam over a coral reef

The butterflies become windblown cinders
Scattering about the canyons
Of a forsaken city
Drifting into the glare of a cracked street light
Peppering my upturned face
With fleeting shadows

In hollow eyed structures ,
Spectral faces whisper offers
With long dead voices and desperate hands
Then vanish into doorways black as tombs

Broken glass glitters in the playground
Where playing is forgotten
I kick the shards aside

And slide my back along the rusted fence
Breathing deep to inhale my last hope

The burning richness fills me
As unhinged eyes roll backwards.
Through webs of glowing veins
I see the black bat burst the net
Wings of taut skin
Waving goodbye to this world

A starving angel leaves my ruined body
Twitching on the cracked cement
To follow him into oblivion

Looking down
The streets dark abyss
Is broken by short tongues of flames
Calling in the helpless moths
And devouring them

Awakening amidst the verdant fragrance of the bemban
I leave the grove on a familiar path
Unsettled by distant cries
Of moths
And men.

Tara Lamberti

How to Make an Inadequate Quilt

My life is loosely stitched together with missed opportunities,
risks I didn't take, men I didn't date
I'm an ill-crafted patchwork quilt
devoid of intricate patterns that weave a story of a life lived
depicted in colorful thread
instead there's a dull grey square where actual London fog should
have swirled around my ankles
a swatch of faded red bleeding for the beds I never laid in with
Jason, Randy, Gary and Elvin
flat patches of sap green for the plateau I remained on
never climbing the mountain mixture of colors, vibrant and strong,
breathing the air from the tree tops
nothing but muted mediocre hues that blend together like
paintbrush water, murky and grim
this is what happens when you remove the "L" from quilt
or hand over the needle to someone else –
it's a sure-fire way to die
wrapped-up in this hackneyed shroud

the frequency of life: love vibrations

floating, floating, floating
on your mind's wave
the frequency of life
vibrates with creation

we are energy
made up of cells
electrons, the smallest part of a cell
is energy, vibrating -
that energy is sound
our own, unique, magnificent song!!!

the music within me
the fabric of life
YHWH's frequency
- our soul song -
  soulful—>wonderful
  dancing in our cells
- love vibrations -

the micro, the macro lens
even my cells sing praises to YHWH!!!!!!!!!
the tree within
the Creator in me

YHWH—>sighs—>
the breath of life
- love vibrations -
of The Spirit
the idea has life
is alive, is alive, IS ALIVE!!!
the idea, the idea
the words
blossom, create
vibrate, vibrate
forms ourselves
reforms our world!
- the frequency of light -

John Lange

Card Wars

It was only recently
That bubble-gum cards with poets showed up.
eBay is crowded; Amazon is busy.
Trading is brisk; auctions proliferate.
Christies and Sotheby's are at one another's throat.

The rage seems to have begun simultaneously
Like plagues of daffodils nodding in the summer breeze
In several places at more or less the same time.
It was an idea, it seems, "whose time had come."
Some, however, attribute the phenomenon
To Hermann Von Horckleschnort,
Poet Laureate of Bridgewater, South Dakota.
But that is controversial.

Competition is intense; trading is fierce.
One Donne is alleged to have gone for two Keats.
Yeats and Auden are neck and neck.
Shakespeares hold steady and Marlowes are starting to be noticed.
Baby Boomers go for the Brownings; Byron is big
with Millennials;
Couples prefer Pope.

Rival companies spring up,

Like daffodils nodding in the summer breeze.
Card wars are already underway.
Vachel Lindsay is in trouble with the NAACP.
Crime enters and flourishes;
Scandals erupt; the market totters;
It requires forensic expertise
To distinguish a genuine Von Horckleschnort
From its brilliantly crafted, insidious counterfeit.

Poetry books now dominate the best-seller lists;
The shelves of poetry sections in book stores yawn emptily,
Like fields newly bereft of daffodils nodding in the
summer breeze;
Libraries are looted for Housmans, Eliots, and Pounds.
Beowulf lives again.

Can I interest anyone here in a vintage Walt Whitman?
It's in mint condition; the edges are sharp; the colors are crisp.
There are no creases or stains.
I am willing to let it go cheap,
But not too cheap.
It's a Whitman.

Linda Leff

The War Closet

Behind a brown wooden door
Faded in color and grain,
Unnoticed, a corner immersed in decades of pain.
Shelved scars of suffering,
Nightmarish scenes, unspeakable words,
Food items urgently placed on a sturdy shelf.

Jars of richly colored coffees,
  assorted pungent teas,
Yellow canned corn, red beans,
  green and orange cans of peas.
Industrial cans of thick red sauce,
Beside cream-colored pasta in every size.
Huge burlaps bags of white rice
   Took up one entire shelf,
The kind you buy in the supermarket on sale.

The closet stood quietly.
Immune to the turbulence behind its door.
My father glares through the wood,
seeing himself with starving men;
  empty stomachs and bloated minds,
  glazed eyes sunken, bungled bodies,
  prolonged lives of dead men.

Unfaded memories, surging over the years,
Always kept the war closet full.

Iris Levin

things

my mother's green leather suitcase is full
it sits in the garage waiting to be emptied
of her things
things taken from the place she died
it sits in the garage waiting
I sit in the garage starring
not ready to unpack
memories of
her things
her last days
of her

Sheri Lynn

burdened, yet determined

In this nest lit
with daybreak's sun,
ease sets our once
everyday habits
Yet, now is no
prosaic day—
though music plays
and windows allow
nature's breath in,
as yesterday
blurs in haste to
past era memoirs
and we wait in
expectant angst—
what will breech your,
our sea's horizon
unknown as to
glory or gloom
remote in our
nests, we let hope guide

John Lysaght

Legacy

Well? *What is your response?*
Did you live a worthy life?---
What can you proffer
That may help your petition?
Have you done enough?

I have pondered the distillate of my time
As a human alumnus,
Inventorying my conscience
And re-assessing my contribution.
My frailties. though abundant,
None bore malice, nor retribution.
My knowledge acquired
Oft evolved into wisdom---
Dutiful to myself,
And shared with others.
I aspired to personal congruence
To cobble a pathway forward,
Mindful not to debase,
But to honor my forebearers.
Although I repine that
I could have done much more---
Been more---
I tried my best.

I hope to be remembered
With a tear and a smile.

Lynda Malerba

Estate Sale

Records for the hi-fi covered in dust
Waiting on chestnut shelves to be adored again
Merlot glasses once stained by red lipstick
Untouched in the cupboard since the house was lit up by life
Strangers parading through rooms
Crushing their soles on the green shag carpet and crimson area rug
Riffling through mother's old handbags, perhaps a treasure of a half unwrapped butterscotch hid in the zippered pocket
A puzzle surely missing a few pieces scattered on the old card table marked 50 cents
Was it worth the risk?
A vase once wrapped lovingly and presented on a special day was now desperate on the mantel, devoid of the flower stems it used to hold so proudly
Praying for a revival in the center of someone else's dining table
A petite wooden chair upholstered in red satin gives a stare of evil from the corner of the basement
Wandering from room to room, level to level, shoppers focused on a deal
Not once realizing that this was where someone celebrated life, raised children
Opened the front door for the first time with hope and anticipation so many years before
Lived out life's joys and heartaches,

triumphs and accomplishments
They would seek sanctuary in their home, away from the outside world
And now the outside world was in here, invading this sacred place for a three dollar coffee pot

Nicholas Malerba

The Sky's Colors

I went out one evening to see the sunset
The sky was yellow, white, blue and red
The beautiful colors shined and sparkled
I went out the next evening,
The sunset more shiny and beautiful
How grateful I am that everyday the sun rises and sets

Maria Manobianco

From Different Views

I pictured the night
you dared to convince
the Professor, I thought
was handsome
to open the gallery
to view his photography

He beamed from all our attention
And when ready to leave the gallery
your back turned, he blew me a kiss

As we descended the stairs
I no longer kept my secret
We giggled, holding tightly to
the railing, amazed by our new
found power and afraid of tripping

Later years, fear and anxiety
our unwelcome companion
when husbands lost jobs
unemployment benefits ran out
doctor's appointments
presented the unexpected

Yes, I remember it all
and miss you

Cristian Martinez

Our Superheroes

Ensuring we are all safe,
defending society with all it takes,
these are the true heroes.
Their uniforms hold the special powers.
Now teachers are asked to defend the classroom,
soldiers are helping other countries in doom.
Police officers keep our streets safe,
firefighters make sure we don't burn down the place.
Doctor's save our lives,
nurses are helping right by their side.
First responders are there in our distress,
helping anyone who could be in a mess.
Without these heroes our world would collapse.
Please take a moment to give praise
to the superheroes who risk their lives every day.
These are the reasons our world is a safer place.

John F. McMullen

Reading The Obits

As I read the headlines on my NY Times
Digital subscription of Friday, July 12, 2019

I saw the following headlines:

Jim Bouton, Author of Tell-All Baseball Memoir 'Ball Four,'
Dies at 80
Walt Michaels, Outspoken Coach of the Jets, Is Dead at 89
Andrew Dibner, Medical Alert Pioneer, Is Dead at 93
Artur Brauner, Producer of Films on Holocaust, Dies at 100

-
You will note the order of the list
I want to be on the bottom of mine

Gene McParland

Dream #87197

I relax totally into my over-sized recliner,
here in the library room
of my dreams

What dream tonight?

An heroic adventure?
A scary thriller?
An all-out horror experience?
Maybe a love tale
Filled with erotic fantasy?
Possibly a psychedelic collage
Of random light thoughts?
So many choices.

But I'll probably go with
An old favorite.
I guess I already knew this though.
It's the same every night.

Dream #87197.

My dream of you and I together.

Ria Meade

Cape Cod

Steamy July evening—oppressive.
I take one of my dogs out for his last break.
Pass my garden privet hedge.
The scent awakens the memory
        of when I was five years old on Cape Cod.

The shingled, rented colonial,
        weathered dark, not painted.
        Wood floors throughout.
My sister Anne claims everything was wood—
        floors, walls, bathtub, toilet seat, kitchen sink.
                Possible, fifty years ago.

A long, narrow, dusty road ran along the beachfront.
Colonies of family cottages dotted both sides.
We six siblings scattered,
        playing everywhere, joined by similar summer kids.
Parents never worried, confident we'd reappear
        when the bakery truck arrived,
the ice cream man's bell rang,
or Wee Packet fried clams were served
in someone's backyard.

So excited, we walked the ribbon of sand and dirt,

to the arcade at this road's end.
Think of it!
Paddle boats, miniature golf,
forbidden games of bingo,
cones piled high with strawberry ice cream.

I bring my guide dog back inside.
Weighted memories come in, too.
Sit down, dwelling on that road.
Maybe it was just a lane,
possibly, fifty years ago.

Was it the loneliness I felt this July day,
the evening's air so thick,
like my impenetrable blindness?
I wept, hard, loud, my animals silent, anxious.
Damn—my nose for filling up
with the smells of the privet hedge,
that perfumed and protected,
each side of that road I knew.

I never thought I wouldn't see Cape Cod again.

Lisa Diaz Meyer

Daytime Moon

Daytime moon
In bright blue sky
The wintertime
Eats you alive
Still you hang there
In half delight
How powerful
How proud
To be seen
From day to night
When the sun cannot
Do as you
And live in dark sky
Without being consumed.

Susan Michele Meyer-Corbett

The Changing of the Guard

Tender moments unfold, quietly
almost unattended on balmy Spring days
approaching dusk in lambent colors, flitting orange,
pinks, the lilac-gray blues of dusk approaching
a lamentation for loves lost in moments of
blazing formidable Sun strokes that leaves one
wonder, in dismay that shimmers, begging for revision,
for new beginnings.
Sympathy displays where earth and sea meet.
We find it in ourselves, the physical part that rises with
unplanned floes and flows of emotion, like the night
suburban teens struggled to find a balance of take and give
that rides a new moon to fine forms of gentle abiding.
This day as families gather in restitution, sailboats praise
the way the harbor wends, its reedy places and craggy corners,
some spots padded with rushes for creature's ease.
The Light reflects in carefree couples, easy like ancient Loves
reliving times past in this Present, graced by regal Swans
& their downy five ducklings paddling after hovering parents,
protective pearlescent feathers rising.

Rose Miller

Close Call

Making my way down the produce aisle
Squeezing avocados, tasting grapes
Intent on finding flawless bananas
Not too yellow, not too green
Finally settling on a bunch
Not perfect, but not bruised
I turn to put them in the cart
And there you are posing at the bakery counter
Whipped cream cakes
Cheese Danish
Rainbow cookies
And you
It's been a lifetime
In the agony of recognition
All that I've accomplished
And all that I've lost
In these desert years vanish
Without a word, you glide off
Head held high
Like the figure skater you used to be
Disappearing into the indifferent audience
Lightheaded, disoriented, I gasp
Unaware I was holding my breath
Too close, too close
Too close a call

Lisa Mintz

Narrow To Wide

The light of positivity
shines deep within your soul
Release all that is not you
Polish your corners,
refine your lens.
For beauty circles all around you,
open the door and let it in
Your eyes reveal the light inside
Beauty, beauty, let it shine
Open wide the door of change,
it's time to expand from
narrow to wide.

There is no secret formula,
just open the door and step outside…

Narrow to wide
The light that you hide
It's time to grow
Narrow to wide.

Procrastinator in Chief

Plenty of time,
March 14th is days away.
I'll get to it no problem,
here's a start, two brilliant sentences.
Gotta make that call,
need to stop to eat.

It's only March 7th,
Rome was not built in a day.
I'll let the idea germinate,
blossom into a piece that will inspire.

Wow, my calendar is cluttered.
I'm neglecting things.
What have I missed?

Write a to-do list.
That's it, that's the ticket
plenty of time to address that,
I'll get to it tomorrow.

What, it's the Ides of March!
Oops, guess I missed the fourteenth.
There's always next year.

George H. Northrup

Collateralized Poetry Obligations

Buy this book!

Sales of poetry books
drive economic growth,
their gross dollar volume
ranking somewhere below
automobiles and smart phones.

Each book purchased
swells employment
in the paper industry.
Manufacturers of printers' ink
expand their factories.
More bookcases
and English teachers
are required.
And, of course, poetry revenue
helps offset the high costs
of unemployment insurance
in the literary arts.

Every dollar spent on poetry
raises government levies
on sales and income,

supporting solar power
and cancer research.

Each poetry book in circulation
edifies on average 2.7 literati,
consumes less than one branch
of an average tree.
When it's useful life is over,
a volume recycled at the power plant
generates enough electric light
to read a sonnet or three limericks.

What are you waiting for?
Buy this book—
it's good for business.
It makes America great again.

Michele Nuceder

The Last Emoji

To all my Facebook Friends
All 1278 of you
I spend way too much time with you
FOMO has consumed my life
And so I must say good-bye
No more clicking and scrolling
Every post, every notification and every link
So in this final post...
Here's a thumbs up for the pictures of your meals
Here's a heart for your children and your pets
Here's a sad face for your losses and disappointments
Here's an angry face for your discontent
Here's a laughing face is for all of your jokes
I wish all of you a Happy Birthday and a Merry Holiday
Have a wonderful vacation and get well soon
Hang in there and keep up the good work
Congratulations and good luck
So as you all send out your shares and your posts
Please know that I'm thinking of you with a big smiley face
And this is my last emoji

Bruce Pandolfo

Reverie

My form is gaunt, limp before this gauntlet
Dawning on me I'm donning daunting expectations
set them high it IS lonely on top,
when will work's worrying stop?
Here I come, ready or not
Jackhammer heart steadily throbs
high-strung-actor-as-I'm-threading the plot
Digesting tests intestines are caught in the Gordian Knot
Rust creaks in genius cogs
Curdled cream of the crop-circular-reasoning-talk
the seasonal thaw moving the seed and the sod
Muse and I? Peas in a pod
Sacrifice (she is my God)
Pantomime pleading for thoughts
a bean for a stalk
Feed find foes fumblin'
tumble tense humble head in the cumulonimbus
accumulate kinship Jack-be-nimblest-
of-all-trade winds and it's kismet.
Balancing on wits on LITerate
matchsticks in a spin-drift
imagining crowd reactions = Jiminy Crickets
on shoulder chips had to grin-and-bear-witness
Fastened with a Mobius strip it's fascinating

as we drafted through these scripts
descriptive magic in these spells and cursive
in encrypted incantations in ink and take this
effervescent effort's essence
transmute it to ululations
you can't mute and you crank this volume up
THANK MUSIC!
Glass half-full yet add volume to it
inspiring: The required inquiring
how queer to find the choir quieting
decidedly with standards as high as these
they're heavenly altitudes
editing refinery, I'm fine and see
a hell of a mountain view!

Marlene Patti

Addicted

We're all addicted
wouldn't you agree?
things favorable
things unseen:

we all want that flavor

the feeling that lingers

we all have our vices

our dark desires too

some may kill you

some are just too good
too delicious to keep
this is the beginning
my addictions ring true

Mary C. M. Phillips

Lock and Key

Often we create our own prisons
sentence ourselves
we are the best prosecutors
but one day when the warden
has failed to show up
a familiar song stirs within
and we remember that the key
is there
snug in our own pocket

JoAnn Phoenix

What I Bought

What I bought: dried beans and extra coffee
Some snacks, cookies, which I hide
Of course, early on, toilet paper
But not a lot…
I bought wine to drink while listening to the news
More canvases, so I could create
Though I have yet to touch those
I bought chicken soup in a box and crackers
In case of illness
Ginger ale and some sports drink to rehydrate
I bought extra tea to help relax in the afternoons
I bought more pens for journaling
The pens dry up fast
Like life, our ink used carelessly
Until the last few drops remain
Which, we finally realize are so precious

Kelly Powell

worlds colliding

sitting on 25a
in setauket, waiting to make a turn left
but make a right turn by mistake
down gnarled hollow road
down a dead end street
a dirt path leads to no way out
beautiful oak trees on either side
block a three point turn
with a split rail and barbed wire
so by driving in reverse
am able to emerge on a smoother,
steadier ashphalt road
passing wild grapes climbing frantically
growing in a circle toward the blue sky
through a rusted chain link fence
and a common dove perched
in the pines

Kathleen Powers-Vermaelen

Arachnid Conspiracy

The arachnid underworld
has contracted me out. Every
spring, assassins sneak in
crawl past thresholds,
hover in archways,
waiting to snipe me
when I pass through.

The hit-spider I found
on my pillow is now
jailed in a mason jar,
yellow with spray starch,
punch-drunk from shaking,
my victory hollow because
others will come.

My friends claim arachnids
don't plan attacks, yet
one evening I found them,
six eight-legged terrorists
circling the hallway light,
strategizing or holding a séance;
I couldn't tell which,

so armed with a flyswatter
and a bottle of hairspray, I
await their next attempt,
Sleepless in Syosset,
enough caffeine in my blood
to power western Long Island.

Molly Prep

Rhapsody

If pasts were poems
our memories would rhyme

the meter, the moments, parallel

IVs beeping in iambic pentameter,
Shakespearian in the sounds
and silences

between

pain wrapped in metaphors
of warring words
to make us soldiers
who fight to survive
ourselves

filled with

allusions to an elsewhere
of Wellness
of After
only a few impossible stanzas away

but first there is

darkness and fear
darkness and fear
darkness and fear
until there is light
until there is hope
until there is now

and now

we must remember

there is power-strength-comfort as we share our pasts,
for a poem repeated becomes a chant
and a chant well-sung
becomes
a hymn

Let us sing together until tomorrow
and then let us sing
again.

Pearl Ketover Prilik

Invincible Then

Whirling hair in convertible rides
striding through fields bare legged
carried in cars with deep voiced boys
convinced that they would
take you home when you
asked and keep their hands.
on the wheel and out of
you and their pants…
The winds of summer tussled
tumbled tendrils of disarray

Legs were neither scratched
nor stung in those summer fields
and despite all warnings to the
contrary
the boys listened
and you were as you thought -
Invincible -
then.

Ben Ray

Ode to Studying

Help.
These words on this page
All coming together.
To form.
Nothing.

I should
Be able to,
Understand this.
But their meaning
Alludes me.

Like the dust
In the wind.
I can not grasp,
All that I need to gather,
From this page.

I can not learn.
When my brain,
Decides,
To not be there.

Barbara Reiher-Meyers

Open 24 Hours

I stopped at a store
in his neighborhood,
wondering what to say
if we met.

Would I dart behind
bread counter,
make a U turn
at the ice machine,
cower in the corner
until he left?

What if I went
boldly to the register ,
purchased my supplies
and feigned surprise
when he helloed?

What if he
ignored me as he did
that last time ?
Would I grab a knife

wipe the butter on my skirt,
proceed to vivisect him?

I think so.

Merri Rose Reilly

Thrones

The shrapnel strikes
Long spikes
Impale your head and heart

You then decide
You will not hide
It's not enough to start

Your mind games
Thoughts change
I'm not allowed to speak

Swallowed pride
It's all inside
Surprised my vocal shriek

It's irritating
You're contemplating
I think you should go home

How dare you say
Today's my day
How dare you throw your throne

The people shout
They want you out
It's an incessant drone

But you won't leave
Hearts on my sleeve
How dare you throw your throne

Mimi 5/18

My Christopher, you say the strangest things to me sometimes, and yet somehow always manage to inspire me with only a few words. Thank you for the pictures you paint with those words. They are beautiful, if sometimes odd. I do adore you and could listen to you share your heart for hours on end. I love you.

Lauren Reiss

Voiceless

Like the "silver swan who living had no note," *
Unsung love is caged forever inside my silent throat.
I envy the swan her elegance and peace;
In my breast strong wings beat frantically for release.
Feathered white wings, tender and warm
Struggle valiantly with their raging storm.
Rising up against their ribcage jail of bone,
A love so beautiful should not remain alone.
The energy of love bursts toward freedom's flight;
The arched jail of bone unyielding to their plight.
Strength slowly ebbs from their wearied tries.
Pain is expressed in their voiceless cries.
Battered and broken, barely fluttering they lie
Unembraced, in their cage they slowly die.
Flightless and unsung these passions must be.
Alone by the shore, waves carry them out to the sea.

*Line from "The Silver Swan," poem and madrigal by Orlando Gibbons, year 1611.

Greg S. Resnick

Loss Of An Elder

To those lost
those young and old
they departed from
this world.
Leaving us
to remember them.

The tears
we shed in sorrow
at their memories
turn to tears of joy.
Remembering the good
times shared
and the moments last
shared.

Knowledge lost to time
forever mourned
never returned.
A mourner's sorrow
is in the wake
covered only by
false joy and hope
from memories

once upon a time.

They leave behind much
for us to remember them by.
A legacy of knowledge
or something as simple as
possession.

We look back on
their lives and think
how great they were
and how they touched our lives.

To lose someone
close to you is hard.
But true friends and family
will always be there
with a shoulder to cry on.

The loss of one wise
can disturb a world.
That loss can come
at random
to anyone.
Even I with
intelligence so broad
cannot foresee
death.

Diana R. Richman

Never Alone

Let's keep our social distance
Remain contained within our home,
Maintain six feet from others
Trusting we're never alone.

Embrace social media connections
Renew relationships via cell phone,
Send texts to communicate daily
Trusting we're never alone.

Wash hands with soap and hot water
Sanitize surfaces where droplets have roamed,
Wear masks to avoid spreading germs
Trusting we're never alone.

Take a solo walk through nature
Enjoy savoring an ice cream cone,
Keep basic supplies stored safely
Trusting we're never alone.

Spend meaningful time with yourself
Be mindful of ways that you've grown,
As you confront this pandemic challenge
Trusting we're never alone.

Telecommuting virtually at work
Each day brings another unknown,
Offering expertise and resources
Trusting we're never alone.

Feel comfort from family and friends
No matter where this enemy is thrown,
Cherish with grace the courage of others
Trusting we're never alone.

An uninvited global experience
Connects us all and lets it be known -
We will help each other survive this
Because we have never been alone.

Allie Rieger

Ghosts

I can fill up a space
with all of me so easily.
A ring, forgotten on the counter.
A ringlet of hair, on your pillow.
The walls could hold echoes of laughter,
the windows a ghost,
a reflection long ago past.
But you will know I had been there.
The atmosphere charged.
Feel the static hanging in the air.
You will feel me,
full.

Al Ripandelli

From Death

An earthly gathering
where amongst sobs and smiles
we celebrate a life and say goodbye.
While in the celestial antechamber
you are received
your heavenly host joyously welcomes you home.

Rita B. Rose

Harvest Moon

Moonlight drizzles across the Great South Bay
kissing our waterfront table at Captree—
Your Blue Moon beer bottle glistens
in Creamsicle beams as does
your aqua eyes… blonde hair… your vanilla skin….
observe the Harvest moon,
I say to you— indifferent— droning on about you.

The unruffled bay embraces the moon
as if it a drop on a spoon;
its carroty splendor splashing across sails, pilings, dunes—
The boat basin is awash in celestial delight.

Oblivious to the summer splendor, you chat of trials
while sipping Belgian white beer
and I— captivated only by sugary wisps
dancing across my hands… my goose flesh— watch
as bright streams caress my shoulders; dewy as warm milk.

I surf the glistening horizon then rise— I leave you for the moon!

Vivian Rose

Adam's Ale

While morning stays awake
the fairies rest
their wings enveloping the textures of the sun
the waves lapping by the feet of
those who love the sea

The constellation envy a chance to burst,
to challenge oxygen's hold on their lungs
they should comply with logic but the
irrationality of love stays firm

Freedom, maybe?
Love, always.
It is binding, it is infinite
In the stars you see love, but I see love in
my grandmother's white braid

as she dives and swims
with authentic expertise as apart of the waves.
Her beginning began here, and her ending,
the last wave to crash over her head will be here
She will accept it, if not already.
For that's what love is, to forever revoke the lost.

Marc Rosen

Tapestry

Caduceus, the twinned serpents along the staff
Runs down the spine, the tails lazing across the ass
Coming to rest upon the quadriceps
A testament to his second chance
The Scales of Libra balance between the snakes' jaws
Justice and rights, his eternal war
His sufferance, his strife, his life itself

Serpents loop and entwine, seven times in all
Each loop, holding an image of the chakras
Each image, a vision of him

Within the Crown, a full moon, bearing a grimace
Its cold, unforgiving scowl and light a reflection
The Monster of Fifty-Nine Moons revealed in its glare
Agonizing wails of a detested child

Within the Third Eye, a smartphone on a bed
The crucial moment of a life almost extinguished
The start of two weeks, alone, unwanted
Fighting for survival as lungs filled with fluid in a hospital bed
Struggling to live as the heart was ravaged by viral assailants
The beginning of years of agony, exhaustion, loss

Within the Throat's loop, a raging bonfire, with huddling masses gathering for warmth
The power of a reclusive orator, one whose words turned a slumbering mass into a raging army
His desperate plea remains silent for himself
Yet for another's sake, the world is at his beck and call

Borne by the Heart, a wheel spoked with Serch Bythols
Each Knot of Everlasting Love holding one leaf in the wheel's center
An endless cycle of love longed for, love offered
Of love never returned, no matter how it might be sought

Proudly found in the Solar Plexus, a raised fist, bearing the black armband
The exclamation of "YP!" emblazoned in white upon its length
Embodiment of the reason he fights, of those he fights for
His reason to live, his reason to survive

Upon the Sacral chakra, the emblem of Mars, wreathed in flames,
Surrounded by a charred heart, barely scorched as the world burns in passion
Love and lust surround this man, yet he himself is hardly moved
None of it has ever been towards him

At the Root, little is there at all
Some grass, and nothing more
No creatures, no large plants, not even a few stones
The man is adrift, unbound

Reborn through modern medicine
Hopeful someone will ask

A. A. Rubin

Sonnet For The First Grey Hair

When I a single silver strand did spy,
Beneath my frown betwixt my tawny beard
My reflection betrayed a subtle sigh,
For the moment had come, which long I feared.
A symbol 'twas of my advancing age--
A sentinel signaling more to come--
Like Dante traveling on his first page--
I realized half of my days had run.
But when you saw that grey upon my face,
You seemed to respect me a little more:
A wise man now, possessed of stately grace,
Future Merlin, Gandalf, or Dumbledore.
What magic then, in a reflection new,
Who sees from a different point of view!

Joseph A. Samoles

Hurt Me

A string of fables
Is all we have left now,
As it was once
A bridge,
Drifting to the dreamland
Of happiness.
We could forget
This nightmare we call
Life,
Live vicariously with
A smile,
And a blush.
I hope to achieve
Such a day where we
Lose the ability to
Hurt,
Yet our path to love,
The circle of life
Does not permit us
To love for
Long.
Now I sit here,
Becoming fragile

By each second,
Looking for another
Force to
Hurt me.
I am clinging on
The string that is
Tearing me apart,
Yet this miracle
Will not
Come,
It will fade
To the other side.
I have watched
The news,
As I absorbed the position
We are in,
The string tears
Harder to scatter
Our fibers.
I take a breath
And I let myself
Go,
Realizing this bridge
Doomed itself,
Like our feelings.

Robert Savino

Reincarnation of Mary Tudor

Bloody Mary was remembered during an unrivaled
reign of terror, striving for reformation.
And now she has returned from the dead,
a mid-Summer predator,
mysteriously, in a human buzz
amongst a swarm circling her target,
sneakily, to get under the skin
and draw blood like soda pop,
to leave a point-of-entry wound
incessantly itching to be healed.
She will persecute with a number of bites.
She yearns to attempt viral execution
before weakening to a death
preempted by life clutches of continuity.

Karen Schulte

Rembrandt's Camera

A bonnet hides my face,
tilted upward in this portrait
of my three year old self
seated on a bench outside
my grandfather's store.

My grandfather sits at one end,
his white spitz dog,
in between,
lit against deepening shadows,
an illumination worthy
of an artist of light and shade.

Grandpa with his white wavy hair
looks straight ahead.
On his lips, a smile
about to happen, stopped
short by some thought
he could only
reveal to himself.

Rembrandt would have been
proud to paint us—
My grandfather with his first American grandchild,

but it was only my father
taking pictures whenever he could
who pointed that box camera
at the precise moment
and snapped us
sitting so peacefully.

Ron Scott

Precious Time

Is this my last sunrise?
Is this my last caress?
Is this my last adventure?
Is this my last story?

If I allow these energy vampires
To invade my consciousness,
Then,
I have wasted precious time.

Barbara Segal

This Summer Night

Katydids knit the distance
between *a* and *b,*
first chorus and second,
nearer and farther.
Their sounds and rhythms
stitch together
a neighbor's trees
with mine.
My old Japanese maple
unfolds its umbrella of stars
over the pond
of slow-dreaming koi.
This summer night
I rise from bed,
pen these words,
think of you.

Leslie Simon

The Flame

a single spark is grace and power
it sees movements of the mind
it reflects emotions buried deep within

it's the tiny dancer
whirling rhythms of the heart
spinning a fire that burns

profound betrayal
twists and contorts in shadows
the flame defines darkness in her heart

her breath, once a sweet whisper
now angry, inhales sickness and disease
billows out an evil stench

without light
darkness and death rots the heart
toxic fumes spew out anger

hate ignites the wick
leaving my spirit
scorched and writhing in pain

my soul cries out

Keith Simmons

Almost A Love Letter

Dear Enchanting Lady,

I enjoyed our momentary glance across the room at last night's office party. Your eyes held a sense of mystery and, I believe, an instant mutual attraction, as opposed to the 3 women in your group who were pointing and laughing at me. But I hope this letter, by telling you more about me, will encourage you to tell more about yourself and that you might offer an evening when I can take you to dinner.

Getting to know me better:

I thought in the interest of clarity I would provide insight into what makes me tick by presenting the results of a recent survey that point to some of my strong characteristics and my very few deficiencies. I sent the survey to over 150 friends, acquaintances and former lovers. The results were at times inspiring, often eye opening, while several ratings left me quite befuddled.

On the basis of the International Relationship Ranking Index (or IRRI) I've been rated an overall 9.3 out of 10 but must admit that, with the onset of aging issues, mental retention dropped an alarming 30% while my ability to attract women above my station in life fell only 2%. My sexual performance factor has fallen to 9.6 (based on my personal observations) while my compassion and forgiveness indices have stabilized at 7.3 and 6.7 respectively. My reliability index slipped again this year. I think I can reliably say that it will slip again next year.

My friends estimated my life expectancy at 11.4 years if I end my drug and alcohol abuse, but would increase to 19.7 if I were to marry someone as stimulating and intoxicating as you ... might turn out to be.

Sincerity came in at 9.1 but drops to 4.0 when I act childish.

Here's one rating that I found most perplexing. It was from former lovers who, as a group, responded "nice guy, but he never understood me".

Where the survey misses its mark is in the lack of questions pertaining to financial security and life goals, things that should be divulged when entering into a new relationship. So let me fill you in by mentioning the cost of my many divorces and my inability to win at games of chance. Of course, current performance is no indication of future results, so I wouldn't let this overly concern you. That being said, there is always next month's social security check to fund our romance.

Regarding life goals, I think it is important to note that since my hip and liver replacements I am a bit more lively and much more comfortable sitting on the couch, watching golf, and eating guacamole dip. Is that a goal??

My most outstanding emotional flaw is my need to learn how to better pretend to be more engaged with you, especially while I am watching football. I'm not even sure if that is possible... unless you were doing one of your 9.7's on me.

Hoping to hear from you!

To our Shared Destiny and a 9.8 romance...

Emily-Sue Sloane

Pop-up Thunderstorm

The thunder that has been bellowing directly overhead
finally lumbers off in pursuit of its lightning-flash prey.
The house's familiar hum
yields to the sound of torrential rain
as it pounds the roof,
cascades over gutters.
Summer's damp heat seeps in
under windows and doors.
Twilight draws the blinds.
Outside, the air smells like fire.
Piercing sirens race up the avenue,
one after the other.
Doused traffic lights add to the chaos.
Our backyard trees hold their leafy canopy aloft.
My anxiety follows the thunder eastward, out to sea.
In a few hours, the house will resume its humming.

Barbara Southard

Retired Men at Cedar Beach

They rush to the entrance of the harbor
when the snappers come in
casting their lines, while scanning
for that tell-tale ripple of water, flash of silver
skittering across the cerulean surface of the inlet,
friends lined up at the sidelines
waiting for the the blues to follow.

When a snapper dances at the end
of a buddy's line they break out in cheers
like they're at a ball game
and the batter hits a home run—
while the guy reeling the snapper in
wise-cracks he's caught a bonito.

Soon the voracious big ones
will come through with the tide,
chasing after anything that moves,
the men ready with their lines
hoping this is their day for a wham-bam strike.

Deborah L. Staunton

Derailed

Everything I do is stitched with its color
W.S. Merwin

Daddy's black suit and white shirt, crisp, neatly buttoned and ucked. His tie, black, wide, sharp at its edges. His face, clean-shaven, melling of Old Spice and toothpaste. His hair, jet-black in loose nglets. His eyes, sky-blue, dark when (he thinks) nobody can see. on, the low-rumbling train whisks him and all the cardboard cut-out hers away through the dense morning fog.

At night, the front door opens, keys jingle. He returns– tie askew, uttons undone, toothpaste and Old Spice lost in a haze of whis- reath. Soon, the train leaves without him and his eyes go dark, ng the light from my own.

Ed Stever

Confined

I'm living in the slum
of my mind, broken bottles,
rusted cans, fish skeletons,
pustulating rats, cockroaches,
maggots, lusting lice,
as a man in a filthy overcoat
and piss-stained pants
sits, leans against
a back alley wall.
He wants out,
out of these confines,
this lurid hell, with all
its demons and spent sperm.
He begs my pardon, begs to go,
and I, of the crooked-tooth smile,
simply croak, "No."

Lennon Stravato

Purpose

You said I'm just like Daniel
in that lions den
but his faith was stronger
so i must be near my end

Well I was born a stranger
and if now it's even worse
I still don't see the danger
so just call off that hearse

I've faced so many burdens
and none did take me down
You shouldn't look so certain
this is my final round

Go bring me your Goliath
with his mighty javelin
I've slayed my share of giants
I'll leave him to the wind

But when the day is over
and distractions are all gone
I'll have to make accounts
for the things I have not done

For there's that greater struggle
that one against our fate
To which so many buckle
and refuse to penetrate

As for me I may be losing
but victory ain't out of sight
so never mind that bruising
I'm still in the fight

Al Strynkowski

We Pray - We Love
We Care - we help
and when that fails
we pray - love - care
and help
For when one broken heart is healed
many broken hearts are
healed

Douglas G. Swezey

#1427 (Messenger of G-d)

For Marilyn

Even my aunt's spell
I won't.
Explain:

Sugar Cookie
Sandies
Snickerdoodles
But
Also:
Peanut Butter Blossoms
Gooey swirled ones
Flat sticky ones
Less a spell I guess –
Christmas
Which she was for me,
So many of us
Now, I live up North, in New York
Where she came from
(Incidentally, you can take the girl
Out of Flushing, but not….)
But gradually grew her family
Further and further south

Until Florida

I grew also up
Took jobs
Got lost in the business of business
But never so for Christmas
Signaled by the delivery of
A package.
A wonder.
A reminder.
A small nudge towards
    Hey, here I am. Take a break
It was
    I didn't forget you, know I am here.
It's
    Partake of this, the body of Christ
    Do this in Remembrance of Me.
Okay, not bread
        More sugar
        And chocolate
        Maybe some sprinkles
Oh, and we can decorate it:
      Let's put these candies between
      And it must be dressed properly
      Yes, even inside the tin.
      Wear a doily.
She feels bad now, but even made
Her son get dressed to the nines
For his football team photo

And so thankful am I when

The first day of Christmas
Arrives
But then, so were the squirrels
Whom thought also
This miracle from up on high
Was for them
Tore open the parchment
And feasted dozens of miracles
Across the lawn
            For me
                    For them
                            The spirit is for all

Oh well, she said
And followed with the timing of a Swiss watch
That's the way the cookie crumbles
And then the contagious giggling
Which made me feel again as a schoolboy
When even in my thirties

The spirit is for all
Yet never so enriched
Until we all sit down
And have a cuppa'
With some cookies
            And family.

Jose Talavera

Happy Bard's Day

Here we are gathered again
Another year of sharing our works
Preparing for weeks
Possibly even months
Yearly tradition grows again

Brining people in from all over our island
And even some from around the world
Regulars and newcomers join every year
Dedicated poets just can't be stopped
Sharing the fruits of our love and labor is what we do

Damn, this is such a great experience
And remember to all our writers
Your efforts make this day possible

Wayne Thoden

Another Day

If chance be got to try again
With thought my mind consumed.
To change the past and end regret
A new day thus be bloomed.

But lessons learned on follies blight
Both good and bad reward.
Give heart and soul their character
For that there's no discord.

While emptiness envelops me
And I'm devoid of will.
To carry on, continuing
That life be not a shill.

But changing that which has gone by
To form a new today.
Would surely end up damaging
In some uncertain way.

So chance I'd take, I do not think
Just put the past away.
And worry not what future brings
For that's another day.

John Jay Tucker

My Father My Son
More Than Memories

Summertime, 1965
I was just a little guy

Feeling butterfly breezes
Blowing across my knees

As I watched my Hero, drive
Rarely having far to go

Lucky to hear
A song or two

From His old Comets radio

I could hardly wait
For my Dad to sing

Along with the hit
England Swings
Like a pendulum do
Bobbies on bicycle
Two by two ...

More Than Memories

Well, singing never
Was my inclination

However, it is the source
Of my explanation

Regarding Grandpa's lesson
In Shared Happiness
Clever, read my fathers lines
In-between Roger Millers rhymes
Which took me years

And the arrival of you
My Son, to detect

Summertime, 1986
I took Rogers tip

And our little family
Made that trip

Across the sea to England
Oh, England did swing

A remarkable place
Rolling mist
Off the cliffs

Of Saint Ives
Poised beneath

Majestic, silver-blue skies
    Gulls in flight

Lined the salt air
As gentle winds
Playfully danced

Through mother and sons
Strawberry-blonde hair

Mermaid tears
Held in Her hands
Make bright, my reflection
Of lovely JoAnne

Vision of Eunice
Amid, lady's lace
Her beautiful eyes
Full of, both hers
And Gods grace

We had been gone
For three weeks

Now home in the states
Visits made early
A few, half past eight

All for a peek
At your rosy red cheeks

You were learning to talk
Holding my hand
You'd run while I walked

To the corner
Of Seaman and Grand

We'd stop, take a long look
As I gave you a lift
You'd watch the leafs drift
Both of us, rambling on
With that babbling brook

Soon, I began to hum
An old tune
Sung by Neil Young
His words, they
Just seemed to fit

In a few years

At the top
Of our lungs

You me and the girls

Would sing it
With, Shared Happiness

Our house
Was a very very
Very fine house

With three kids
In the yard

Life never seemed
To hard
Everything was easy

Because of you John

My wonderful son

J R Turek

Faithful

for Tammy
December 18, 1965 ~ March 2, 2020

You were one of only a few
I had ever met, and though I do not judge,
I could not conceive of disbelief,
never rationalized
the concept of an atheist.

I prayed for you often, told you frequently,
you chuffed it off as wasted words
for an unworthy soul.
Blessed with faith since birth,
I continued to pray for you.

You lost your son before I knew you,
before he was two, and on Christmas Day.
The celebration of the Savior's birth, a day
you denied thereafter in anger. *Why?*
Why my son? Why why why?
Any hope of faith drowned in your tears.

An acrid divorce, a separation
from your daughter, and along with her,
severed your time with your only grandson.

Your pain festered, boiled up and over
and then, you found your soul mate.

Long lost smiles returned to glitter your eyes
with abiding love; your daughter called,
a hope to reconcile, time with a baby now grown
to a little boy; a solitaire slipped on your finger,
promises of everlasting forevers.

And somewhere in there, you found God.
Began to pray for all you had, good and bad,
all you survived, all you wished for.
You filled a bucket of tears, regret mingled
with gratitude.

Never questioning God's will,
I prayed prayers of fortitude for you
sprinkled with gladness. Then the diagnosis,
dire, lacking longitude and we both prayed.
You stumbled, fell a few times into an abyss –

Why? Why now when I have all I need,
all I ever dreamed of? Why why why?
God answered with challenging treatments,
ups and downs, and finally
all clear.

You prayed, never alone, yet never sure
of tomorrow, an instinct to not trust
what's yet unwritten. No nuptials date set,

not rushing, and then the sky broke open,
chunks fell to cancel the next act.

Heart aching, I pray alone; you smile down,
me missing you – friend, secret keeper, soul sister.
God is patient; He waited for you to find your way
to him through adversity and love, and now
you’re safe in His embrace.

Vertulie Vincent

Thank you

Towards this spring of love
Scraped with your "I love you"
I shall lean over every day
To quench my thirst
To this parterre of love
Scattered with your "I love you"
I shall go every day
To let me wander
In this sanctuary of love
Designed with your "I love you"
I shall snuggle every day
To comfort myself
Thank you for this bliss
From the bottom of my heart
I want to shout out
How much I love you!

James P. Wagner (Ishwa)

A Final Victory
For Uncle Paul

It had been 9 years
since I first learned
how to play chess.
And for 9 long years
I endured your traps
your tactics
your countless victories.
.
I'd lost track of the minutes, or hours
spend sitting across the chessboard
on that picnic table
on the side of the house
in all types of weather.

This was a chilly November evening
as I cautiously moved my Knight from behind my King's pawn
I thought of my recent games
against opponents in tournaments.
I was 13 now...
in a whole new league,
had been to chess club,
studied books,

had won trophies.
But you were the man
who taught me how to play...
and for 9 years,
Uncle Paul, you had beaten me
without fail.

Every time I thought I had the edge
you pulled something unexpected,
something I hadn't seen coming...
but I remember this cold November night
as you examined the board in front of us,
looked up at me,
then back at the board,
weighing your options...
finding few...
until finally,
you knocked over his King,
extended his hand
a hand much larger than mine
and proclaimed me the winner.

Was this a fluke?
A mistake?
I couldn't believe it.
We played another 4 games that night...
and in each one,
I emerged the victor.
3 by surrender,
2 by checkmate.

"You have done well, young grasshopper" you said
in that dramatic voice you liked to do...
"The student has surpassed the master..., good job pal..."
Pal,
is what you always called me.

Of all the games I have played since then,
I'd never felt more proud
than I did that night.

And hearing from Grandpa
about how you called him the next day
to tell him how I had beaten you
I knew you were proud too.

I wouldn't know the significance of those 5 games
until later on.
Not because they were the first games I ever beat you at Chess
but because they were the last we ever played.

Less than two months later
in early January,
like a guardian angel
who had fulfilled their purpose
you left this world...
at only 48 years old.
Too early,

much too early.
I still had so many things left to learn from you
and we still had so many more games
left to play.

Jillian Wagner

Crisis and Opportunity

In the early days of the COVID panic,
when people were buying out supermarkets, battling over toilet paper,
and terrified to step outdoors for fear of getting sick,
I too foud myself having to brave a panicked grocery store.
That spring day was rainy, grey and just dismal all around;
having to stay late at work again wasn't fun either.
But after getting what I needed and free to step outside and remove my already-familiar mask,
I saw that the rain had stopped.
The day was still grey, the air was still damp, but painted in the sky
was a huge bright rainbow.
Sitting in my car, I paused and looked at the colors for a bit,
reflecting on something I had learned years ago.
"The word for crisis in Japanese is also the word for opportunity," Sensei had said
during one of my *many* karate classes.
While it would be more truthful to note that the kanji for "crisis" is made of the words "danger" *and* "opportunity," Sensei's words came back to me.
And while a rainy day is hardly matches a pandemic, I found myself wondering

how many people were so focused on the current crisis that they missed the opportunity to see something beautiful.

Margarette Wahl

Anything, but Wasted Youth

for Erik-Michael Estrada

His talents supersede my expectations.
Two years ago tonight
saw him for the first time.
I thought he was twenty years old,
in fact he was nearing forty.
Wearing navy bandanna on his head
in a red and black flannel,
he appeared more a gang member than performer.

His youngness resides inside the sounds of his voice.
Dancing keeps him fit.
His dark hair of curls of Puerto Rican
mixed with Italian blood carry his irresistible charm.

His eyes hold a sparkle like stars
with brown, almost black pupils
resemble a night's sky.
Whenever I look inside them,
I place wishes.

Herb Wahlsteen

Rejoicing Joyce

The dusk unfolds its prussian blue and carmine
gown. Venus slowly strides down from her bright
throne. Saffron smiles begin to beam. White wine,
crushed from star-grapes, has made the moon's head light.

Once silk-draped lakes are wearing purple fleece.
A flock of hidden, cabbalistic quails,
with low-sung songs, is lulling solemn peace.
Orange-velvet sails on cloud-ships catch high gales.

Tonight, I trace bronze paths through woods filled with
pied, fragrant flowers to a plum-hued pond.
There lives my love: a dryad from a myth,
well-graced with gifts by beauty's brilliant wand.

I'll enter this enchanted land of splendor
to live an obscure life with love forever.

Virginia Walker

Discovering Truth under Golden Arches

I wanted Caesar Salad with Caesar Dressing,
the only eatable in the smeary twenty-four
hour serving all comers. Nose stud, mango mouth
totaled me three eighty-five. God! The senior price!
I calculated if I could drop her and teen crew
with one machete blow, my plastic fork split
her mango lip before 911 could be called.

To be sure I asked her the age for senior price.
Mango called out a number and a zero smile,
noting only my coffee was on the discount.
The teen crew smiled raspberry, fuchsia and poppy.
Well, I was on a fast approach but not there yet.
I knocked five years off and demanded the full price.
The line behind me had increased from five to nine,

but still I had to explain to the counter broad
her miscalculation. Sometimes, intoning, I look
tired when I forget my lipstick, like today,
too rushed for a doctor's appointment. Mango grinned.
A somewhat clean table, my napkin unfolded,
I tear open the fat gray bag of aged dressing,
sip coffee, and stare at my mouth's coral imprint.

George Wallace

Biography of an Imaginary Man

an imaginary man appeared on the high forehead of the mountain
below which he was born

it was a wrinkle of time, it was the spring of 1885

a piccolo sounded like heroic wind the moment he appeared, he
was dressed as a dark angel and had a long beard

and in his hair the scent of sage burning in the sun, perhaps a hint
of nutmeg
at his feet a pantheistic sea which covered everything

he was the neptune of that sea, his flesh was brittle with scales, his
breast composed of the soil of many different islands

he was solid and real as a continent and furthermore erotic --
especially when he was not sad or separated from his sanity by
having been made mad with the world

his mother in the morning was illuminated like a flower

his father at dusk was a disappearing act in sea mist

his children were the afternoon sun in a grove of olives, the light
of which glows like apollo in love with his own music

this was a lifelong ambition of his, and had to do with an unde fined and inescapable sense of personal destiny
nobody believed him when he told them about his lineage or manner of birth

there was a rumor that went around, an intimation of sexual ambiguity (though the reader will no doubt discern the difference between human observation of circumstance and circumstance itself)
he had his loves and elevations; he had his traditions; he had his low moments and a weakness for the fantastical, which came over him from time to time like a ghost

he was a big drink of water all right

he drew himself out of a well with an old oak bucket and lay there a long time watching his own reflection floating on the surface

this did not surprise him in the slightest

he was a metaphor that keeps turning in upon itself without regard to ulterior motives
in time death defeated itself in the grave of his hands and he lived on, he never died -- which is why the gods, like rats on a sinking ship, abandoned him

in recent years he has developed a taste for the literary

it is this and only this which sustains him

Angela Werner

When Left Is Right

If turning left is correct,
Then left is right,
Am I wrong?
And if turning left is incorrect,
Then left is not right,
And I am wrong,
Am I right?
And if I am wrong,
And I say, "I am wrong,"
Then I am right,
Because I am wrong,
Am I right?

Jack Zaffos

You Have Poetry in Your Soul

Flow through the air
like a bird
if you feel the winds
on your back.

The winds that glide
through space
known by a reflection
on the surface of a pond
that you see with your sensitive eyes.

When you see
these ripples in the water,
that is your calling.

You have poetry in your soul.

Thomas Zampino

Last Time

You were a baby.
There was a last time that it wasn't strange when I kissed
your toes.
You were a child.
There was a last time that I held on tight as I walked
alongside your bike.
You were a high school student.
There was a last time that I helped you with your homework.
You graduated from college.
There was a last time that I expected you to return to this place.
You made a home with the love of your life.
There was a last time that I would ever be first in your thoughts.
You and I have both grown older.
There will come a last time that I will ever look upon your face.
I will always love you.
There will never be a last time.

Donna Zephrine

New York Borders

New York has many boundaries and borders.
Many think of the City and Manhattan when they think of New York State, but there are so many areas and beauties to the state.
There is upstate New York, which is more rural, with farms, agri culture, and beautiful sights from mountain tops.
It is impressive that you can drive 6 hours north of Manhattan and still be in New York State but in a completely different area.
New York City is divided by borders into 5 boroughs; Manhattan, Brooklyn, the Bronx, Queens, and Staten Island. Each borough with something different to offer.
Even those boroughs have borders within them of areas or districts that can be so different from one another.
New York City is filled with educational institutions and Universities. It holds two large, well esteemed Universities.
Down town holds New York University, while Columbia University is uptown. Even those two areas are distinct in their own ways.
The Universities have their borders to create campuses for their students.
Over the years parts of the city have become inhabited by certain racial, ethnic, or religious groups.
These borders are created socially rather than geographically, but it is interesting to see how people of similar faiths or ethnicities group themselves together.

While those communities are nice because they bring people together these socially formed boundaries separate people by race/ethnicity and religion.

Borders can bring people together but also separate them.

There is "China Town" where many Asian groups come together and bring their culture to the city.

Parts of Harlem fill with the Spanish and African American cultures.

"Little Italy" is where you will find the smells of Italian foods and festivals.

There are areas more heavily populated with the Jewish religion as well.

Woodside, Jackson Heights, Queens has a heavy Pakistan and Indian population.

New York City is a melting pot and though the city brings all these people together in one city they are separated by the borders created by dividing into separate areas.

On September 11, 2001 all borders and boundaries of New York were broken by the tragedy that hit New York. All New Yorkers felt the heartache as their beloved city was under attack.

It did not matter what part of New York you lived in, where you were from, or your ethnic background, New Yorkers wept when the towers were hit. Tragedy can break boundaries in that way.

About the Authors

Lloyd Abrams, a long-time Freeport resident, is a retired high school teacher and administrator and is an avid recumbent bicycle rider and long-distance walker. Lloyd has been writing short stories for over thirty years and poems for almost a dozen years. His works have been published in more than three dozen anthologies and publications. www.lbavha.com/write

Sharon Anderson is published in many international and local anthologies, was nominated for a Pushcart prize, and has four publications of her own poetry with a fifth to be released soon. She serves on the advisory board of the Nassau County Poet Laureate Society, the advisory board for Bards Initiative, and is a PPA host at Oceanside Library.

Rose Anzick is the proud mother/grandmother of poets Kate Fox and Rebecca Fox. She has been writing since her mid-20s and has been a regular contributor to *Great South Bay Magazine*. Her second love, and hobby, is photography. She is honored and excited to have her poetry included in this anthology.

William H. Balzac is the author of three books of Poetry: "The Wind Shall Hear My Words," (2008) "The Stars Will Speak Them," (2012) and "The Same Page"(2019) He has also been a contributor to the Suffolk County Poetry Review (2019 & 2020) & The Bards Annual (2019 & 2020)

Antonio Bellia (Madly Loved) is a renaissance man who has traveled many paths, a man of deep sentiment drawn to performing arts, who has acted and danced throughout his lifetime, and always compelled to express his emotions and experiences in the form of poetry. He is translating his poems from Italian into English.

Cristina Marie Bernich holds a Master's Degree from Teacher's College Columbia University. She is a pediatric speech, language, and feeding pathologist for children with medical challenges with advanced certifications in her field of study. She writes in her spare time to process all she has witnessed working in the homes of young children and their families.

Thérèse M. Craine Bertsch's work is included in "*Visions and Vocations 2018*". Catholic Women Speak, Bards Suffolk County Poetry, and more. Poetry is her conversation with the reader giving voice to all that is human. She is a mother to 5 and has 8 grandchildren, and is a therapist, clinical director and program/staff developer.

Author **John Anthony Brennan** comes from County Armagh, Ireland. He left his beloved, sacred green isle many years ago to explore the world and has been island hopping ever since. He now resides in New Rochelle. NY

Alice Byrne is a mother and grandmother who has written poetry since she could write. Alice maintains a clinical psychotherapy practice in Huntington, New York

Carlo Frank Calo the grandson of Sicilian immigrants, a husband, father and grandfather. He was born in Harlem, raised in the Bronx projects and is retired on LI. When not fishing, playing poker, counseling TBI survivors part-time or babysitting his grandchildren, he enjoys writing eclectically. 1170boy@optonline.net

Paula Camacho moderates the Farmingdale Poetry Group. She is President of the NCPLS www.ncplsociety.com. She has published three books, *Hidden Between Branches, Choice, More Than Clouds;* and four chapbooks, *The Short Lives of Giants, November's Diary, In Short,* and *Letters.*

Lynne Cannon is from Northport, NY. She writes poetry and has also completed two novels she hopes to publish soon. She is extremely pleased to be part of the great poetry community on Long Island, and also to be included in this volume along with her daughter, Julia Menges.

Caterina de Chirico makes her home in Northport with her kids and furry friends . You can find more of her musings at Fineartamerica. com / CateChirico

Anne Coen is a retired special education teacher whose venture into performance poetry was purely accidental. Assuming incorrectly that attendance was being taken, she promptly signed the clipboard. The rest is history. Anne's work has been published in many anthologies, such as Bards Annual and the PPA Literary Review.

Joseph Coen is the other half of a poetic duo with his wife, Anne, and an aspiring painter. He is the father of a free spirit and senior airman. He has been published in *Bards Annual 2015, 2016, 2018*; and *PPA Literary Review #19* and *#20*.

Jamie Ann Colangelo is a Christian, living on Long Island. She is the mother of twins, Liane and Christopher, now adults. She is the author of From The Father's Heart - A Book of Poems and Suggested Gifts To Inspire, Encourage and Bless Those in Your Circle of Influence. She found her passion for poetry at the age of 12 and now enjoys using her gifts and talents to share God's love and encourage others onlife's journey.

Jane Connelly has won numerous awards, most recently *1st Place* in *Performance Poets Association's 2020 Literary Review.* She is on the Advisory Board of the *Nassau County Poet Laureate Society Review*, and has published in *The Avocet*, *Bard's Review*, *Nassau County Poet Laureate Society Review, Oberon,* and *Performance Poets Association's Literary Review.*

Lorraine Conlin is the Nassau County Poet Laureate Emeritus (2015-2017) Vice-president of the NCPLS and Events Coordinator for PPA. Her poems have been published nationally and internationally in anthologies and literary reviews.

Ushiku Crisafulli is a chef, poet, playwright, actor, performance artist, musician and founder of the OpenMind Collective. His most recent publication "Litany of Varied Experiences" was published by Local Gems Poetry Press in New York and he's currently overseeing their Buzzin Bards project in Manchester, England.

Max Dawson works full-time with adults with mental illness. Dawson is better defined by his interests in The *Civil War, The Transcontinental Railroad,* trains of that very era, day to day life in that very era, medieval history, and most importantly, writing. He has written for *Back-Row Cinemas*, a site reviewing movies and films—old and new.

Anthony DeGennaro is a research scientist living and working in Long Island, New York. He received his Ph.D. in Aerospace Engineering from Princeton University in 2016.

Debbie De Louise is a librarian at the Hicksville Public Library and the author of eight novels including the five books of her Cobble Cove cozy mystery series. She lives on Long Island with her husband, daughter, and three cats. Check out her website at https://debbiedelouise.com.

Arlene Diaz is a poet and writer who has been working on her craft for the past seven years. She was recently encouraged by her three children to start sharing her raw poetry on social media after becoming widowed in 2013, as they believed her healing process would inspire and resonate with many. She is currently working on her first book, Pen to Paper. Find her work on social media: @pentopaper381

Sharon Dockweiler runs a weekly creative writers' workshop at Brentwood Public Library. Her poems, essays, and fiction tackle tough subjects with wit and flair.

Joseph Drouin-Keith is a high school student from Greenlawn, N.Y.

Mike Duff was born in New York and raised in Queens. He attended Michigan State University and London City College. He resides in Freeport.

Peter V. Dugan, former Nassau County Poet Laureate (2017-19). Mr. Dugan co-edited and formatted the a poetry anthologies: Writing Outside the Lines, LI Sounds 2015, and Leaves of Me . . .. He also hosts a reading series at the Oceanside Library, NY and an open mic at Sip This Café in Valley Stream, NY.

Alex Edwards-Bourdrez's poetry has won regional contests and has appeared in *Bards Annual*, *PPA Review*, and other anthologies. Following careers in teaching, public relations, and disability services, he is retired and co-manages the local food pantry in Northport. His chapbook, *Transformations*, is due out this fall.

Donna Felton is a single mother of two kids, Akinda 23, and Niah who is ten years old. She is currently working on a masters degree at Queens College in Literacy. Donna Felton is a substitute teacher at Park Avenue School in Westbury. Her first collection of poetry is entitled In High Regards. She is know in Westbury as the poet in Residence.

Meilssa E. Filppelli is a Long Islander, born and raised. She writes because she must and because she finds a unique comfort, strength, and voice with each penned word. You can find her poetry in *Poets to Come*, an anthology in honor of Walt Whitman and his legacy.

Adam D. Fisher is the author of poetry, stories and liturgy. In addition to publishing many poems in journals and magazines, he has published four books of poetry: Rooms, Airy Rooms (Writers Ink, Cross Cultural Communications and Behrman House), Dancing Alone (Birnham Wood/ LI Quarterly), Enough to Stop the Heart (Writers Ink) and Hanging Out With God (Writers Ink.) He was Poetry Editor (2006-2014) of the CCAR Journal, the Journal of the Central Conference of American Rabbis.

Denise-Marie Fisher has been a involved with the online writing community since 1999, and helped created "Poetry Tag Group" which ran poetry workshops nightly, for over ten years. She has two adult sons, had owned a business for 30 plus years, and is now a marketing consultant. Denise has been included in several Bard's editions.

Kate Fox is a mother, breast cancer survivor, and award-winning author of the collections ***My Pink Ribbons, Hope, Liars, Mistruths and Perception***, and ***Angels and Saints***. She is the host of The Kate Fox Show. www.katespityparty.com

Glenn P. Garamella was raised in Douglaston, NY, attended Queens College; BA in Philosophy, MA in Counseling Psychology; NYU Lifelong meditator, student of Eastern Religion and Spirituality. Married, lives in Huntington, NY. Son lives in Boston, MA.

George S. George is the son of Cypriot immigrants who came to America in the 1920s. He was born in Brooklyn, NY, and as a child lived in Virginia, North Carolina and New Jersey. He was graduated from Rutgers University in 1963, taught English and eventually went into advertising. He currently lives on LI with his wife, Joan.

Tina Lechner Gibbons has been writing for more than 50 years and was recently published in *The Suffolk County Poetry Review*, and *Poets to Come*, Walt Whitman's Bicentennial Poetry Anthology. She is currently working on her collection of poems and hopes to be publishing a chapbook in the near future.

Jessica Goody is the award-winning author of *Defense Mechanisms: Poems on Life, Love, and Loss* (Phosphene Publishing, 2016) and *Phoenix: Transformation Poems* (CW Books, 2019). Her writing has appeared in over four dozen publications, including *The Wallace Stevens Journal*, *Reader's Digest*, *The Centrifugal Eye*, *Phantom Drift*, *The High Window*, *Event Horizon*, *The Dime Show Review*, *Chicken Soup for the Soul*, *The Seventh Wave*, *Third Wednesday*, *The MacGuffin*, *Harbinger Asylum*, and *The Maine Review*. A frequent contributor to *The Creativity Webzine*, Jessica is a columnist for *SunSations* Magazine and the winner of the 2016 *Magnets and Ladders* Poetry Prize.

Aaron Griffin is a 31-year-old Long Island native who is currently working as a warehouse club clerk, and self-training as an advertising copywriter. He was priced out of LI and fled to Charlotte, North Carolina. He writes fiction in his spare time. He likes Pokémon and trains.

Valerie M. Griggs earned an MFA in Creative Writing from Brooklyn College (1985). She enjoys being part of the vibrant poetry community on Long Island. As a singer/songwriter, she has recorded three original music CDs. Currently, she works as a writing center consultant and adjunct English Instructor at Molloy College.

Daryel Groom has had numerous poems and short stories published in college literary magazines such as Nassau Community College *This is Big Paper* and Molloy College's *Curiouser Curiouser.* In addition, she has published articles in the Nassau Community College *Vignette.* Currently, she has a poem entitled "Mermaids" being published in Long Island's *Odyssey* Magazine and the poem "Phantoms" in the 2020 edition of Nassau County *Voices in Verse.* Furthermore, she contributed to an online publication focusing on ancestry with a piece entitled "My American Ancestry".

Maureen Hadzick-Spizak is a retired Language Arts Teacher, an award-winning poet, and author of two poetry books: *A Bite of the Big Apple* and *Yesterday I Was Young.* Publications include *Whispers and Shouts, Bards Annual,* and *Sounds of Solace.* She's a member of Farmingdale Creative Writing and Poetry Groups and The Bards Initiative.

Geneva Lillian Hagar lives in Melville, NY. She has a BA in Fine Arts from Stony Brook University. Geneva has published three books, The Folk Art Poet,Moon Flowers and The Silver Tree. She has been honored by being acceptedin the Bards Annual 2019, The Long IslandQuarterly 2019 and the Suffolk County Poetry Review 2019.

J Peter Hansen has his M.A. in Music Education & Music Theory from Hofstra University & Queens College NY. He is President of SLI (Songwriters of Long Island) and a Board member of The Long Island Blues Society. He is an affiliate of The Songwriters Hall of Fame, BMI, NSAI (Nashville Songwriters Association Inc), NYSSMA and NAFME. He is an Adjunct at 5 Towns College and a retired PS Music Teacher.

Michele Harber is a lifetime resident of Queens, and a lifelong lover of poetry. She is a frequent contributor to the popular FanStory writing site, where she's taken first, second or third place in 75 of their writing contests over the past year-and-a-half. She has also read her poetry at the Kew and Willow bookshop. Her goal is to find a publisher for one or more of her picture book manuscripts, several written in verse.

Robert L. Harrison is an award-winning poet, photographer, and playwright who has been active in the arts scene on Long island for the past twenty-five years.

Sheila Hoffenberg has been published in *The American Poetry Anthology*, *PPA Literary Review 2016*, and *Nassau County Poet Laureate Society Review 2018*. She won an honorable mention in the Princess Ronkonkoma Adult Poetry Contest and has been a member of the Long Island Writers' Guild since 2012.

Arnold Hollander publishes a quarterly magazine, *Grassroot Reflections*. He has poems in various anthologies. His poem, "A Penny For Your Thoughts," was nominated for a Pushcart award. His poems and short stories are in the online magazine, *Bewildering Stories* and he keeps a blog at www.arnieh.webs.com.

Cheryl Huneke was born, raised, married and continues to live on Long Island with her husband Artie. Her first poetry debut publication in Bards Annual was in 2018. The Suffolk Poetry Review was her second poetry debut publication in their Poets to Come-a Poetry Anthology in 2019. She enjoys reading and writing poetry along with creating drawings, paintings, and relaxes taking photographs, listening to music or designing quilts. Her creative inspiration comes from her family, friends and the wonderful beaches and quaint towns of Long Island.

R. J. Huneke has had poems published in numerous literary magazines and books, including *Unleashing Satellites*, *Suffolk County Poetry Review*, and *Bards Annual*. As a finalist in the 2018 Local Gems Press NaPoWriMo Chapbook Contest, *American Political Asylum*, his first book of poetry, received publication in 2019.

Maria Iliou is an autistic artist, poet, actress, director, producer, advocate, and host. Maria's been published in *Perspectives, Bards Annual 2011-2016,* and *Rhyme and PUNishment*. Maria is host for *Athena Autistic Artist*, which airs on public access tv and hosts the radio show, *Mind Stream The Movement of Poetry and Music*.

Larry Jaffe is the author of four books of poetry: *Unprotected Poetry, Anguish of the Blacksmith's Forge, In Plain View, 30 Aught 4,* and the soon to be published *Man without Borders*. He was co-founder of Poets for Peace (now Poets without Borders) and is a judge for the epic Arizona Poetry Contest.

Lauren Jayne is a singer-songwriter with a remarkable gift for storytelling and a knack for crafting poetic lyrics. At the beginning of 2020, Lauren decided to pursue a career in creative writing. As a native Long Islander, she credits the local libraries to her literary advancements because they have become a place of support providing access to a selection of online educational resources. Currently,

Lauren is a resident of East Northport and enjoys walking around Northport Village Park to inspire artistic thinking.

Ryan Jones began writing at an early age and believes it to be the best way to express one's thoughts and ideas. Ryan's topics of interest include nature, human and natural history, mythology, and personal and collective experience, all of which are influential to his writings. Ryan holds a bachelor's degree in English with a master's degree in childhood education, and works with children by profession.

Daniel Kerr CPA, PhD, teaches accounting at St. Joseph's College and Suffolk County Community College and is also a lay minister in the Episcopal Church. His work has been recognized by the UN (Doing Business in a Multicultural World) and the Steinhardt School of Education at NYU (2009 Business Education Alumni of Year).

Zach Klebner is a writer, filmmaker, and comedian from Long Beach, New York who believes in the power of art to heal and transcend lines of division. You can follow him on Twitter (@ZKlebaner) and Medium (@zach-klebaner) where he shares his thoughts and connects with other creatives across the globe.

Carissa Kopf is an inspiring poet who has published her first poetry book called Coffee, Wine, and the Magic of Words. She also has a romance novella called Time For Me available worldwide. When not teaching or dancing her finger across the keyboard she enjoys her time reading, cooking, and planning or tending to her garden.

Mindy Kronenberg is the author of *Dismantling the Playground,* a poetry chapbook, *Images of America*: *Miller Place*, a pictorial history/

illustrated chapbook of poems, *Open*. She is co-editing an anthology, *Paumanok Rising Again: Long Islanders Reflect on Climate Change.* Poet, writer, critic, and professor at SUNY Empire State College.

Melissa Kuch is the author of the Amazon best-selling YA fantasy series, *The Hypothesis of Giants.* Nominated as one of the Best Authors of Long Island, Melissa is an advocate for literacy and continues to inspire the next generation of authors through her writing workshop programs. Born and raised on Long Island, Melissa currently resides in Massapequa Park with her husband Michael and their daughter Lily. You can follow Melissa on FB/IG @melissakuchauthor and her website www.melissakuch.com

Joan F. Kuchner (Ph.D. Psychology, The Univ. of Chicago), Former Director of Child & Family Studies, Dept. of Psychology, Stony Brook Univ., is enjoying her retirement as it has given her the time to play with her four grandchildren and to write poetry some of which has been published in the *Bard's Annual* and the *Oberon Poetry Magazine* and featured in the *Southold Library Poetry Gallery*.

Tara Lamberti is a psychic and poet who lives in Head of the Harbor with her beloved Golden Retriever, Chewbacca.

Billy Lamont is a multimedia poetry performer who has performed on national television a number of times, including MTV and Joe Franklin Show, toured and performed with rock festivals such as Lollapalooza, and appeared on major radio stations across the U.S. He has three books of poetry and eight poetry with music CD/digital download releases. His latest December 2019 book of poetry edition: *Words Ripped From A Soul Still Bleeding: Poems For The Future*

Edition is available at Barnes And Noble and Amazon as a paperback or as an eBook.

John F. Lange Born in Chicago, in 1931. Radio and film writer; sergeant, AUS; story analyst, Warner Brothers Motion Pictures; technical editor and special materials writer in the rocket-engine industry; and teacher of philosophy, primarily in the City University of New York.

Linda Leff Although quietly writing poetry for many years, inclusion in *Bards Annual 2020* is her second published poem. Highly motivated to pursue her inner voice, poetic inspiration can be acquired from hikes in the woods, archery and fly-fishing. The sounds and smells of the sea shore is a particular joy.

Iris Levin, a retired educator, now works as a photo archivist for Nassau County. She writes with open eyes and open heart seeing her poetry as snapshots of life. She has been published in Whispers and Shouts, Nassau County Poet Laureate Review, Bards Annual, Sounds of Solace, Paumanok Poems and Pictures of Long Island, and Performance Poets Association of Literary Review.

Sheri Lynn launched her first poetry and photography chapbook *Nature's Breath*, accompanying postcards and website BreatheInsights.com in 2019. Her works were published by NCPLS, PPA, Bard's, the 911 Museum Artist Registry, LIWG's The Odyssey and, upcoming in August, by Chicken Soup for The Soul and North Sea Poetry Scene Press. Recently accepted into the LIAG (Long Island Author's Group), Sheri is grateful to LIWG, NCPLS, PPA,

PIN, LILA, DBP, Bard's, LIAG, LIPC, family and friends for encouragement in this fortuitous writer's adventure!

John Lysaght is a poet and fiction writer who began honing his craft while in college, graduating in 1968 with a degree in English and Classics. He went on to achieve a Masters in Social Work John seeks to invite the audience to participate in the experience of the word in real time...

Linda Malerba has been writing for over 30 years. She likes to explore different topics in her writing and she is open to inspiration from limitless sources.

Nicholas Malerba is in the first grade.

Maria Manobianco published three poetry books and a Young Adult Fable. She was an Archivist for NCPLS 2007-2015. In 2015, Maria received a pushcart nomination for a Sonnet, "On Meditation." She earned a BS from NYU and a MA from Adelphi University.

Cristian Martinez is a 13-year-old 8th-grade student at Ronkonkoma Middle School and award winning poet. He has been published in Bards Annual 2018, 2019 and 2020, PPA 23rd Annual Literary Review, Suffolk County Poetry Review 2019 and 2020, Mankh's Haiku Calendar for 2019 and 2020 and the Long Island Quarterly. Cristian won first place in the Princess Ronkonkoma Awards competition for his poetry and prose submissions in 2018 and 2019, PPA 1st place for a haiku submitted, and 1st in the Mid-Island Y 2019 Contest. He was awarded for his poem, "Glimpse of Tomorrow" with recognition as the Grand Champion for the Walt Whitman Birthplace

Contest and published in their anthology. *Glimpse of Tomorrow* is Cristian's first book. He has been mentored by Robert Savino for the past two years which has helped Cristian fine-tune his craft. Cristian also loves to play soccer.

John F. McMullen, *"johnmac the bard"*, is the Poet Laureate of the Town of Yorktown, NY, an adjunct professor at Westchester Community College, a graduate of Iona College, the holder of two Masters degrees from Marist College, a member of the American Academy of Poets and Poets & Writers, the author of over 2,500 columns and articles and 10 books, 8 (poetry), and the host of a weekly Internet Radio Show (*300 shows to date*).

Gene McParland (North Babylon, NY): is a graduate from Queens College and possesses graduate degrees from other institutions. He has always had a passion for poetry and the messages it can convey. His works have appeared in numerous poetry publications. He is the author of "Baby Boomer Ramblings, a collection of essays and poetry", and "Adult Without, Child Within",a collection on poetry celebrating the child within. In addition ,he also acts in local theater and videos, and has written several plays.

Lisa Diaz Meyer The poem DAYTIME MOON was self published by independent author, Lisa Diaz Meyer for her award winning book ALL ROADS DESTINED. She proudly hails from Nassau County's south shore where she lives with her husband, children and rescue cat.

Susan Meyer-Corbett is a LI poet with a hope to further creativity as a healing modality for all ages. As a Holistic Counselor she brings a range of modalities to integrate choices for reestablishing personal power in a confusing world. She is a multi-cultural person who sometimes writes in Spanish, and appreciates many mythic traditions.

Lisa Mintz is a multi-media artist in the fields of writing, photography, and pottery. She has led professional development workshops to promote focus and mindfulness through creativity. She lives in Dix Hills with her husband, and is a mother of three and grandmother of one.

C R Montoya CR Montoya has written a series of children's stories narrated by Papa The Happy Snowman. Publishing began in May 2020. He has a curious mind and is a student of nature. Running on trails is a source of inspiration. CR is an avid reader and enjoys challenges. Visit Papa at papatherhappysnowman.com

George H. Northrup has been President of the Fresh Meadows Poets in Queens, NY since 2006 and is a former Board member of the Society that selects the Nassau County Poet Laureate. His chapbook, *You Might Fall In*, was published in 2014 by Local Gems Press, and his latest collection, *Wave into Wave, Light into Light: Poems and Places*, was published by International Psychoanalytic Books. George was President of the New York State Psychological Association in 2009, and served on the Council of Representatives that governs the American Psychological Association from 2012-2014.

Bruce Pandolfo, Long Island native, is best known by the moniker "AllOne" under which he's released 7 off-kilter rap & poetry albums independently and toured extensively in grassroots fashion. Most recently he's released a book of true crime storytelling, songwriting and poetry called "This Is Criminal" and an EP, Halcyon Wonders, with his folk band Almost Elijah. He is currently pursuing a degree in Journalism from Stony Brook University and recording his 8th AllOne studio album, Emotionauts.

Marlene Patti is a Chilean wife, mother, disability rights advocate and a human who wishes to inspire others through her writing. She hopes to start a non profit to help her community with accessible housing and reasonable accommodations. Follow her: @marleneiskey.

Mary C. M. Phillips is a caffeinated wife, mother, and writer. Her inspirational essays have appeared in numerous bestselling anthologies. She blogs at CaffeineEpiphanies.com and can be followed on Twitter @marycmphil.

JoAnn Phoenix has been writing stories for over 20 years but recently turned to poetry as her genre. She'd like to give a tip of the hat to Tim O'Brien's The Things They Carried for inspiring her poem, What I Bought. JoAnn thanks her friends and family for their support in her writing journey.

Kelly Powell is a poet from Long Island.

Kathleen Powers-Vermaelen earned an M.F.A. in Creative Writing & Literature at Stony Brook Southampton. Her work has appeared in *The Bangalore Review*, *The Write Launch*, *Trouvaille Review* and other publications. She teaches literature and writing at Suffolk County Community College.

Molly Prep is a Huntington writer, reader, library clerk, fitness instructor, and life enthusiast. She loves words. She can be reached at mollyprepwrites@gmail.com

Pearl Ketover Prillik is a poet/writer/psychoanalyst; her writing includes several nonfiction books, editor of a post-doc psychoanalytic newsletter, and editor/participant of 2 international poetry journals. She lives on a barrier island on the south shore of LI, NY with DJ, her husband extraordinaire and Oliver, the humanoid cat. http://drpkp.com

Ben Ray is a dyslexic, non-binary writer(he/they pronouns). They live with their parents and brother. Ben will be graduating college with a degree in computer science in the spring of 2021. Along with writing poetry they write fanfiction, under a different name, and make cosplays from scratch. His writing is often in some way derived from life experience, be it his own, or as they are a strong empath, that of others.

Barbara Reiher-Meyers was the LI poetry matriarch; her weekly newsletter kept the poetry community celebrating the art of poetry. She was a board member of LIPC and TNSPS; she coordinated events for Northport Arts Coalition and Smithtown Arts Council and conducted poetry workshops. Barbara's poetry continues to inspire. RIP.

Lauren Reiss is a poet, author, artist, and retired educator of the blind. Her writing has been published in Bards Annual (2018, 2019,

2020), Performance Poets Association 24th Annual Literary Review, and Nassau County Voices in Verse. She is currently writing a book on healing for Balboa Press, and is certified in several forms of energy medicine.

Diana R. Richman, Ph.D. licensed psychologist, has been in private practice for over 40 years. Listening to stories shared by souls, authoring self-help publications, writing rhymes for special occasions since childhood, and playing the cello in community orchestras evoked the desire to express her soul's voice through the musical language of poetry.

Al Ripandelli was raised in Kings Park, NY. He has published in several collections since his introduction in *Bards Annual 2016*. He is also the author of a poetry chapbook, *Hearts Window.*

Rita B. Rose is an award winning poet, author and playwright. She has performed her works for colleges, organizations, social programs and on stage. She is the recipient of two Bards awards and is currently Long Island LGBTQ Poet Laureate

Vivian Rose has been published in five works, Eloquence, and Accomplished of the American Library of Poetry, Leaves of Me, her school's literary magazine, The Key, the Nassau County Anthology, Voices in Verse, and the 2020 Poetry Marathon's Anthology. She was also an attendee to the Literature conference of Champlain College in Vermont and was accepted to the prestigious Bread Loaf conference at Middlebury College. She is apart of the poetry mentoring program started by Peter V. Dugan and Gladys Henderson, and her mentor is Judy (JR) Turek.

Marc Rosen is the Treasurer of The Bards Initiative, editor of *Chaos*, and Lead Editor of *Stonewall's Legacy*, and a magnificent bastard.

A. A. Rubin's poetry has appeared in publications such as Bards Annual, Rhyme and PUNishment. A winner of a Writers Digest award for rhymed poetry, he can be reached on social media as @TheSurrealAri or through his website, aarubin.wordpress.com.

Joseph Samoles is a naturally creative person – he has been interested in poetry and the arts ever since he was a little kid. Now he is slowly putting his mark on the creative world, and he hopes to tap into people's minds with his works. He is currently a student at SUNY Old Westbury for Visual Arts.

Robert Savino, Suffolk County Poet Laureate 2015-2017 & current Bards Laureate, is a native Long Island poet, Board Member at the Walt Whitman Birthplace and winner of the 2008 Oberon Poetry Prize. Robert is the co-editor of a bilingual collection of Long Island Italian Americans Poets (*No Distance Between Us*). His books include *fireballs of an illuminated scarecrow* and *Inside a Turtle Shell*. As a mentor he enjoys being the key that unlocks doors of creative minds.

Karen Schulte is a retired social worker and therapist who began writing in grade school and, since retirement, has had her poetry published in a number of journals and anthologies including, Long Island Quarterly, 25th Anniversary Edition, Poetica Magazine, Paterson Review, Bards Annual, PPA Literary Review, NCPL Literary Review. Her collection of poetry, "Where Desire Settles," won first place in the Writer's Digest 2017 Annual Contest for a self-published book of poetry and recently her poem, "Displaced,"won honorable mention in their national poetry contest for 2019.

Ron Scott currently serves as Executive Vice President to the Nassau County Poet Laureate Society. He also serves on the board of The Long Island Authors' Group as Membership Chair. This reflects the two hats he shares as an author. Not to be remiss, he credits the Long Island Writers' Guild for its collective input in the development of his two novels, *Face of the Enemy* and *Twelve Fifteen.* Ron's work has appeared in various poetry anthologies throughout the region, one in particular resulting in a 2016 Pushcart nomination. He has been featured in several public TV interviews focused on the ongoing plight of Vietnam veterans.

Keith Simmons is a Long Island based writer and singer-songwriter. He serves on the board of the Folk Music Society of Huntington and has assumed the added role of videographer-editor in support of virtual concerts during these pandemic times.

Leslie Simon is a recently published poet and a retired elementary school teacher. She is also an avid quilter for which she is combining this art form with poetry to publish a book. It is unique, in that poems are illustrated by a corresponding quilt. The quilts tell the story of each poem.

Emily-Sue Sloane's poems have appeared in journals and anthologies, including Amethyst Review, Avocet, Bards Annual 2019, Literary Review of the PPA, Long Island Quarterly, and Suffolk

County Poetry Review. Her poem, "Something's Not Right," won the 2020 CAW award for poetry.

Barbara Southard currently serves as Suffolk County Poet Laureate from June 1, 2019-May 31, 2021. Aside from poems and stories published in various journals and anthologies internationally, she has had two books published by Allbook Books: *Remember* (2008) & *Time & Space* (2020). This will be her last year of teaching poetry at Walt Whitman Birthplace, leaving her with many warm memories.

Deborah L. Staunton's work has appeared in The New York Times, Pretty Owl Poetry, Gallery & Studio Arts, Sheepshead Review, The MacGuffin, Six Hens, Literary Mama, and others. Her work was featured in HBO's Inspiration Room exhibit in New York City and her collection of poetry and prose, Untethered, is currently under consideration for publication. She is a member of the International Women's Writing Guild.

Ed Stever Bards Laureate 2015-2017, poet, playwright, actor, and director, Ed Stever has published 2 collections of poetry, *Transparency* and *Propulsion* and *The Man with Tall Skin.* He compiled and edited *Unleashing Satellites: The Undergrad Poetry Project*, and is one of the editors of the *Suffolk County Poetry Review.*

A native Long Islander, **Lennon Stravato** is a poet, screenwriter, and former foreign policy contributor for The Hill newspaper in Washington, D.C. His writing deals with the intersection of faith and despair, eternity and temporality, meaning and meaninglessness.

Douglas G. Swezey received his B.A. in English and Art History from Stony Brook University, has written as a journalist for many weekly newspapers, was Managing Editor of *Government Food Services Magazine* and author of *Stony Brook University: Off The Record* (College Prowler, 2005). Currently, he serves on the Board of Directors for the Bard's Initiative and Long Island Poetry Collective. He is also the co-founder of Super Poem Sunday.

Wayne Thoden is a Gymnastics Instructor, Writer, Artist, Photographer Stand-up comic, and Web Designer, featured on Authors Den, The Years Best Poetry and is the Author of the book Fright Time Stories. Wayne was also a $10,000 winner on Americas Funniest People.

John Jay Tucker A husband, father and grandfather while in retirement enjoys substitute teaching at Lawrence Woodmere Academy, yoga, hiking and attending poetry events. Published in several PPA Literary Reviews.

J R (Judy) Turek, 2019 LI Poet of the Year, Superintendent of Poetry for the LI Fair, Bards Laureate 2013-2015, an internationally published poet, editor, workshop leader, and 23 years as Moderator of the Farmingdale Creative Writing Group; she has 2 Pushcart Prize nominations. She was named a 2017 NYS Woman of Distinction. She is the author of *Midnight on the Eve of Never, B is for Betwixt and Between, A is for Almost Anything*, *Imagistics,* and *They Come And They Go.* J R, The Purple Poet, lives on Long Island with her soul-mate husband, Paul, her dogs, and her extraordinarily extensive shoe collection. msjevus@optonline.net

James P. Wagner (Ishwa) is an editor, publisher, award-winning fiction writer, essayist, historian performance poet, and alum twice over (BA & MALS) of Dowling College. He is the publisher for Local Gems Poetry Press and the Senior Founder and President of the Bards Initiative. He is also the founder and Grand Laureate of Bards Against Hunger, a series of poetry readings and anthologies dedicated to gathering food for local pantries that operates in over a dozen states. His most recent individual collection of poetry is *Everyday Alchemy.* He was the Long Island, NY National Beat Poet Laureate from 2017-2019. He was the Walt Whitman Bicentennial Convention Chairman and teaches poetry workshops at the Walt Whitman Birth-place State Historic Site. James has edited over 60 poetry anthologies and hosted book launch events up and down the East Coast. He was named the National Beat Poet Laureate of the United States from 2020-2021.

Jillian Wagner earned her BA in Creative Writing from Dowling College. She is an active member of Fanfiction.net and is working on her collection of short stories entitled *13 Dark Tales.* She was one of the founding editors of *Conspiracy*, a genre fiction magazine at Dowling College. She is a certified paralegal and sits on the board for the Bards Initiative.

Margarette Wahl Special Ed Teacher Aide and Poet from Long Island. She is published Anthologies and three chapbooks with Local

Gems Press. She's a huge fan of Erik-Michael Estrada, Bronx-born member of the boyband O-Town whom her poem is written for.

Herb Wahlsteen was a finalist in the *Yale Series of Younger Poets* contest, placed 3rd in the *Writer's Digest* 77th Annual Writing Competition: Rhyming Category, and has had poems published in: *Long Island Quarterly,* the *Great South Bay Magazine*, *The Lyric* magazine, *Paumanok Interwoven, Suffolk County Poetry Review, Bards Annual, Form Quarterly, Bards Against Hunger, 13 Days of Halloween, Poets to Come, The Hands We Hold, String Poet* (2 poems translated from the French, 2 poems translated from the Spanish), *Pratik; A Magazine of Contemporary Writing,* and *Measure* magazine.

Virginia Walker, PhD, taught writing and literature courses at New England and LI colleges. She is the co-author of the poetry book *Neuron Mirror* (with Michael Walsh). Her poems have appeared in *Poets 4 Paris*, *Suffolk County Poetry Review*, *The Light of City and Sea*, and the *Humanist.*

George Wallace is writer in residence at the Walt Whitman Birthplace, author of 37 chapbooks of poetry, and a LI-based poet who travels internationally to present his work. Winner of the many international distinctions, including the Orpheus Prize in Plovdiv Bulgaria, he was Suffolk County's first poet laureate. George edits Walt's Corner (The Long Islander Newspaper), Long Island Quarterly, Poetrybay and is co-editor of Great Weather for Media's annual anthology.

Jack Zaffos is a retired Therapeutic Recreation Specialist. He is the author of *Songlines In The Wilderness*, and *Meditations Of The Heart*. Publications include *PPA Literary Review, Bards Annual,* and *NCPLS.* Known as The Calendar Guy, he curates the PPA monthly calendar. His works have been characterized as Contemplative Poetry.

Thomas Zampino is an attorney in private practice in New York City. He and his wife have raised two daughters, four cats, two dogs, and various other domesticated creatures over the past three decades. He formerly blogged at Patheos and now writes reflections and poetry at Grace Pending. One of his poems was published in Bards Annual 2019. Poetry is his second act!

Donna Zephrine was born in Harlem New York and grew up in Bay Shore, Long island. She went to Brentwood High School, graduated from Columbia University School of Social Work in May 2017 and currently works for the New York State Office of Mental Health at Pilgrim Psychiatric Center Outpatient SOCR (State Operated Community Residence). She is a combat veteran who completed two tours in Iraq. She was on Active duty Army stationed at Hunter Army Airfield 3rd Infantry Division as a mechanic. Since returning home Donna enjoys sharing her experiences and storytelling through writing. Donna's stories most recently have been published in the New York Times, Writers Guild Iniative,The Seasons, Lockdown, Qutub Minar Review, Bards Initiative, Radvocate, Oberon, Long Island Poetry Association and The Mighty. Donna has participated in various veteran writing workshops throughout NYC

The Bards Initiative

A multi-purpose poetry project, The Bards Initiative is dedicated to connecting poetry communities, while promoting the writing and performance of poetry. The Initiative provides avenues for poets to share their work and encourages the use of poetry for social change.

In addition, the Initiative aims to make use of modern technologies to help spread poetry and encourage and inspire poetry, particularly in the younger generations. It is the core belief of the Bards Initiative that poetry is the voice of the people and can be used to help create a sense of sharing and community.

www.bardsinitiative.weebly.com

www.bardsinitiative.com

Local Gems

Local Gems Poetry Press is a small Long Island based poetry press dedicated to spreading poetry through performance and the written word. Local Gems believes that poetry is the voice of the people, and as the sister organization of the Bards Initiative, believes that poetry can be used to make a difference.

www.localgemspoetrypress.com

Made in the USA
Middletown, DE
17 November 2020

24208862R00139